The Gender Crisis: Real, Natural or Imposed... this book. It is a topic many are afraid to touch, yet, it is a topic that should be dealt with in this season. It is like a voice crying in the wilderness, but it is a strong voice. This book is revelation of the truth. A must for Pastors and Leaders. There is a real crisis and Apostle Vernon Duncan is one of the major voices speaking out concerning the current crisis that is challenging spirituality in societies around the world.

Apostle Dr. Ricardo Vincent,
CI Director – Trinidad and Tobago

The Gender Crisis: Real, Natural or Imposed? presents God's truth on His design of the man and the woman. The subject is treated robustly by the author in a spirit of love. I commend this book to those who seek to stand on the word of God and not be distracted by the babel of human opinions. Thanks Apostle J. V. Duncan for another decisive book, written from a heart that loves truth, righteousness and peace.

Dr. Emily G. Dick-Forde FCPA FCMA
Responsible Governance Specialist
Skype: Emily Dick-Forde

If you are looking for a book that would take you through reasoning that provides a firm foundation for policy and personal decisions, promoting right thinking and right action on this important subject, you have found one

Dr. Kathleen James,
President, Caribbean College
of the Bible International. (CCBI)

This book is enlightening, a great read, nothing short of riveting! It is a book that should be used to spur conversation and healthy debate on the issue in question in every educational and intellectual sphere.

Alicia George Jackson (JD, LEC)
Attorney-at-Law

This book on the Bible's viewpoint on the "Gender Issue" is important information on the current discussion of gender. This side of the discussion has to be heard along with any other talks and opinions on gender because it literally affects everyone of us, and how we live our lives. This issue may perhaps even affect our afterlife...or does it? Read Apostle Duncan's book to find out how this Gender Issue/crisis affects us as individuals and to help you understand the Bible viewpoint, should we have to discuss it rationally with others. It takes nothing away from the fact that they "shall know we are Christians by our love"

Dr. Rhonda Lynch-Watts,
Medical Doctor and Christian
for over 20 years.

It is often said there is nothing like an idea whose time has come. This book, therefore, is timely because it is a response to the many unanswered issues surrounding the gender chaos; prophetic because the wisdom of the Holy Spirit is fully demonstrated throughout its presentation; and accurate because of its scholarly representation of the truth regarding the global gender crisis. This book is highly recommended for the genuine seeker of truth.

Rev. Desmond Austin,
President of the Trinidad and Tobago
Council of Evangelical Churches

THE GENDER CRISIS
REAL, NATURAL OR IMPOSED?

APOSTLE J. VERNON DUNCAN

Zakar Productions TNT Ltd. Arima, Trinidad West Indies

The Gender Crisis: Real, Natural or Imposed?

Copyright © 2019 by Apostle Vernon Duncan

All rights reserved. No portion of this publication may be reproduced, stored in a retrieval system, or transmitted in any form or by any means, electronic, mechanical, photocopy or otherwise without the written permission of the author.

All Scripture otherwise stated taken from the New King James Version of the Bible

© Copyright 1962 Thomas Nelson, Inc. Used by permission

Cover Design/Artwork by: Robert C.J. Waldron

ISBN: 9798622884115

Author Contact:

Email: devencounter@yahoo.com

Tel: 868-766-0723

P.O. Box 4848, Arima, Trinidad, West Indies

Printed by Amazon.com

Also by

APOSTLE J. VERNON DUNCAN

Beyond Tehilla: The Worship Experience

•

The Five Laws of Generational Curses: Uprooting Them

•

The Zakar Man: Male Man in Full Flight

•

The Ultimate Baptism: With the Holy Ghost and Fire

•

Kingdom Wealth: The Power to Get It

•

Have You Commanded Your Morning?

•

Press Into the Glory Until: 7 Incredible Pathways to Victory

•

Taking Your Nation Through Personal Evangelization

•

Come Buy Without Money: Advanced Techniques in Kingdom Financing

CONTENTS

Acknowledgements..VIII

Foreword..IX

Preface..XI

1. Introduction..15
2. Demystifying Sex And Gender..23
3. The Creation Account..29
4. Nature's Evidence Of God's Creative Mandate............37
5. The Driving Force Behind Gender Change...................51
6. The Current Feminist Agenda Vs. The Creation Account........65
7. The Spirit Of Jezebel: Male Emasculation In Historical Perspective..75
8. Who Is Stealing Our Fathers?..95
9. Assumed Gender Types And Inevitable Consequences..........107
10. The Discrimination Smokescreen................................117
11. What Then Is The Purpose Of The Law?....................127
12. Homophobia Really A Clever Red Herring................135
13. In Defence Of The Faith..139
14. Know The Truth And Nothing But The Truth..........163

Bibliography..167

DEDICATION

This book is dedicated to all millennials who must be told the truth so that they would be free to help navigate the next generation away from error into their God-given destiny.

ACKNOWLEDGEMENTS

First of all, I am grateful to God Almighty for commissioning me to write this book. He is the God of truth and he hates falsehood; it is an abomination to Him.

I am also thankful to Attorney at Law, Alicia George-Jackson, for her careful and critical scrutiny of this script; she also did the Foreword for this book. Thanks also to Ms Dabrielle Nurse-Lewis who was part of the editing team.

Thanks to Dr. Emily Gaynour Dick-Forde, former Government Minister of the Republic of Trinidad and Tobago, for her scholarly advice in one way or the other.

Thanks to Ms Hyacinth Griffith and other members of Lawyers for Jesus, Trinidad and Tobago, who have been a source of encouragement over the years.

I wish to acknowledge also the support of Rev. Desmond Austin and the Trinidad and Tobago Council of Evangelical Churches together with other national Church leaders for engaging in appropriate defence of the truth over the past decade or so.

To the pastors and members of Divine Encounter Fellowship Ministries International, your listening ear, your encouragement, intercession and cooperation deserve fitting recognition.

Thanks to Ms. Liz-Ann Aguillera and Mr. Robert Waldron (cover design and layout) for the preparatory work in publishing this book.

Finally, I must pay tribute to my wife of forty-four (44) years, Joycelyn, for the green light to go ahead and release the truth for the next generation. To my children, Simone, Verneille and Curtis, thanks for your invaluable moral and spiritual support.

FOREWORD

I have the distinct honour of writing the foreword to this insightful, revelatory and edifying book! However, before I do so, let me re-introduce you to the author. He is an Apostle, Teacher, Senior Pastor, loving Husband, Father and Author of many other books. He is also my Spiritual father, a man whom I have known for ten years and admire immensely, mostly because he 'walks the talk', is humble and a true leader, always leading by example. He can be stern at times and his expectations high, but it's only because he anticipates nothing but the best from those whom he shepherds. He has demonstrated to us time and again that he hears from and is beholden to our Heavenly Father.

Thus, the content of this particular work is not at all surprising, as I know the author has been burdened by the issue, has sought God about it and it is clear that God has answered him; and has done so directly from the Throne Room, using the pages of this book as the vehicle by which we are all to know God's mind on the matter.

As we look around our world today, we see that several nations are in conflict and financial ruin. Humanity seems to have taken a nose-dive for the 'pits'. But, nothing has affected and continues to affect us on a societal level as the issue of same-sex relations and this 'break-out' crisis regarding gender. Inextricably, they have propelled societies into a dark place from where we could only return by God's intervention. As Believers in Christ Jesus, we know that the world, in Jesus' own words, is once again 'in the days of Noah' (Matt. 24:37) and "the days of Lot" (Lk. 17:28). Our hope, however, lies in God

What this book does for us is prepare the reader to "give an answer" to those who would challenge our worldview on the topic. It biblically, spiritually and strategically answers the question of: "what was God's original intent for mankind," and scientifically outlays how God in His wisdom designed our bodies to function.

The book does not fall short; it tells us, by looking at the Word of God, science and real life examples, exactly what God expects from the human race in general and from us who believe in Him in particular.

This book is enlightening, a great read, nothing short of riveting! It is a book that should be used to spur conversation and healthy debate on the issue in question in every educational and intellectual sphere.

It is my humble and intense belief that God Has spoken here; He has informed us of His Word, His Will and His Heart through this author and by extension this book: 'The Gender Crisis: Real, Natural or Imposed?' Read on to obtain the answer!

Alicia George Jackson (JD, LEC)
Attorney-at-Law

PREFACE

This book, *The Gender Crisis: Real, Natural or Imposed*, is written from a place of deep concern and personal responsibility to provide a text that presents the truth about our Creator's intention when He made us male man and female man at the beginning. I have lived long enough to know that the unimaginable is now being entrenched the world over. The word gender is in danger. This word, which historically meant sex, and embodied just two choices, is now being redefined and re-presented to us based on the subjective opinions of individuals and how they view themselves and the world. To be completely honest, it appears, and it may well be, that our very minds are under attack. Many are asking: What is truth in a world where subjective choice is institutionalised and imposed on others?

Indeed, how are we to respond to what we know is a great deception and a departure from God's design and intention, yet presented as human and legal rights to which we are being asked to bow down? It has always been my focus to present God's truth in a manner that is pragmatic and applicable to important life experiences and everyday decision making. In this book, with the lens of Biblical truth, I take you through reasoning that provides a firm foundation for policy and personal decisions, promoting right thinking and right action.

I have a responsibility as an Apostle and Prophet of God to speak the truth and nothing but the truth. Truth may seem to be offensive at times, depending on whom it confronts and what it does to his or her ideology or worldview. Notwithstanding, Jesus admonishes us in these words: "And you shall know the truth, and the truth shall make you free" (Jn. 8:32). Freedom through God's truth is in fact deliverance from bondage, that same bondage that leads one to the deception of making one's own choice regarding gender identity.

This book explores the foregoing issues in more detail, and endeavours to exercise the author's right to "conscientious objection" in a very constructive and enlightening manner. By the way, the foregoing terminology was officially recognized as a human right by Pope Francis in September 2015 on his return flight to Rome after his visit to the United States.

When asked by reporters to give his candid position on the question of government officials, like well-known Kentucky anti-gay marriage clerk, Kim Davis, who "cannot in good conscience" abide by certain laws in discharging their duties, the pontiff publicly said, in part:

> I can say that conscientious objection is a right that is a part of every human right. It is a right. And if a person does not allow others to be a conscientious objector, he denies a right... Conscientious objection must enter into every juridical structure because it is a right, a human right. Otherwise we would end up in a situation where we select what is a right, saying, 'this right that has merit, this one does not.

This is the right that I exercise in this book; so that this work is not intended to cast aspersions or derogatory sentiments on any group of people in an effort to discriminate against them.

Thus, this scholarly work should not be interpreted as hate literature, but rather the dispatching of this author's human right to speak the truth based on his inner convictions and his understanding of God-ordained precepts for the good of humanity.

The reader reserves the right to reject its contents or accept as the case may be. That too is your human right. It is my firm belief that God has directed me to write this book so that the truth will be told, and that you, the reader, will be set free from the great deception that is seeking to penetrate the psyche of this generation and generations to come.

1

Introduction

We live in a gender-confused world. Howbeit, it is a confusion that appears to be completely self-inflicting, emerging mainly from the preposterous notion that gender is not what it was traditionally made out to be. There is a deliberate effort to remove gender from its original roots in order to fulfil a well-orchestrated humanistic agenda. Much of the confusion seems to be meted out on societies around the world by those who are caught up in this gender melee for their own purpose. It is clear that there is no empirical or scientific (DNA or otherwise) evidence to verify their new definitions and concepts. It is all speculation and literary manipulation, laced with intellectual dishonesty and unscrupulous power plays by the power brokers of our day. But there is a God in heaven, the greatest Power of all, and He is still in control.

Is There a Gender Crisis? Is it real?

Exactly what is a crisis? A crisis is a state in which certain acute circumstances have developed, which would require critical decision-making. It is a volatile point in a process when a difficult decision has to be made, a crucial period of time in a life situation.

In the face of this definition, one should not find it implausible that we are in a gender crisis. Yes, there is one. Is it real? Certainly, it is. When you see the male man, the leader of the family, surrendering his manhood and increasingly losing his identity as head of the household, as father and husband, deviating from his necessary roles to guide, guard and govern his household, you know there is a gender crisis.

Moreover, when you see men, although endowed with all their masculine attributes, burning in passion for sexual partners of the same-sex, and likewise women with all their feminine beauty gravitating to other females for sexual fulfilment, you know the crisis is real and it is no small one. It is almost as if there has been a mental or psychological flip-flopping of basic human reasoning and behaviour. Something has gone drastically wrong; civilization lies in danger of self-destructing in the process. The homosexual lifestyle has the potential to reduce fertility rates drastically and render human civilization extinct in a few short years, if we are not careful. An initial fall-out, where the advocated lifestyles become a societal norm, could well be a drastic reduction in the labour force or human resource required to power our economies, owing to falling fertility rates

The Prognosis and Diagnosis

I am glad that the Holy Bible, in the book of Romans chapter 1, verses 18-27, is on top of things here and gives us a clear prognosis concerning this present state of affairs in our world. This enables us who have eyes to see to make a proper diagnosis of what is happening presently in our world:

> For the wrath of God is revealed from heaven against all ungodliness and unrighteousness of men, who suppress the truth in unrighteousness, [19] because what may be known of God is manifest in them, for God has shown it to them. [20] For since the creation of the world His invisible attributes are clearly seen, being understood by the things that are made, even His eternal

power and Godhead, so that they are without excuse, [21] because, although they knew God, they did not glorify Him as God, nor were thankful, but became futile in their thoughts, and their foolish hearts were darkened. [22] Professing to be wise, they became fools, [23] and changed the glory of the incorruptible God into an image made like corruptible man—and birds and four-footed animals and creeping things. [24] Therefore God also gave them up to uncleanness, in the lusts of their hearts, to dishonour their bodies among themselves, [25] who exchanged the truth of God for the lie, and worshiped and served the creature rather than the Creator, who is blessed forever. Amen. [26] For this reason God gave them up to vile passions. For even their women exchanged the natural use for what is against nature. [27] Likewise also the men, leaving the natural use of the woman, burned in their lust for one another, men with men committing what is shameful, and receiving in themselves the penalty of their error which was due.

More would be said about Apostle Paul's prognosis during the course of this book.

Jammed Sexual Signals

Sexual signals seem to have been jammed or fouled up by some mastermind. The God-ordained roles of men and women have gradually whittled away in many quarters; some men are becoming more and more effeminate, seeming to have lost their sense of masculinity as God made them. Some women, on the other hand, whether by reaction, or by a similar masterminding of their conscience and conviction, seem to have been gripped by the same fang. Gender is no longer regarded as consisting of a simple duality of male and female types, as God created us (Gen. 1:27), but is now seen as a spectrum of forms. Many sexual and gender terminologies are now being conveniently redefined or invented to match certain appetites of men and women, many of which are clearly against the laws of nature or biology, and ultimately, the laws of God.

Many nations are now under severe pressure from multilateral institutions to alter their moral, ethical and spiritual laws. These are the very laws that have kept human society along a normal growth path from time immemorial. Instead, humanity is now faced with instability and chaos, even being threatened with extinction, in this mad rush to promote a proliferation of self-centred and imprudent appetites and behaviours. Our children and older youth are being coerced into rebellion against God's creative order and nature itself, for which there are grave consequences, both in the short-run and long-run.

In 1 Samuel 12:15, we read:
> However, if you do not obey the voice of the Lord, but rebel against the commandment of the Lord, then the hand of the Lord will be against you, as it was against your fathers.

We are indeed at a critical point in the history of mankind; the world is changing rapidly before our eyes, and it is quite alarming. Hard and unpopular decisions are required by the morally-minded and God-fearing ones among us, the Church in particular. We are custodians of the truth and we cannot compromise. God is on our side and He will fight for us. Jesus has assured us: ". . . and on this rock I will build My church, and the gates of Hades shall not prevail against it" (Matt. 16:18).

Is this Gender Crisis Natural?

The next question that one must ask is: "Is this gender crisis natural"? And the answer is clearly "No, it is not." It is for the most part concocted and promulgated by way of notions that are furiously antagonistic to the laws of nature.

The tenets of this crisis are humanly created and are unreal for the most part. Many of the new recommendations and redefinitions advocate sexual practices and designations that contravene the very biological laws governing the human person.

In fact, some social advocates are presumptuous enough to claim that several time-tested scientific or biological findings may be in error.

In the process, there have been strong appeals to human rights laws, but even the latter have been misconstrued and misapplied. Human rights are inalienable rights that naturally accrue to one simply because he or she is a human being, regardless of race, ethnicity, religion, sex or any other rank or standing in life (various online sources). Therefore, it is absurd to engage in practices that are contrary to the science of nature and yet appeal to human rights for protection.

Human rights are erroneously used in modern times as being synonymous with equal rights; however, they are not necessarily the same. While equal rights refer to all people having the same entitlements, liberties, rights or opportunities under the law, there is some inherent deception in this concept, if careful attention is not paid to the definition of "rights" itself. It is undeniable that this word "rights," as originally intended, is derived from the root understanding of what is true, correct, moral, proper, just or appropriate. Thus, one cannot, by the very nature of human rights, regard something as a human right if that thing is contrary to the truism of nature, thereby making it wrong

The problem with "equal rights" is that if one simply, or rather simplistically, accommodate everybody's wishes without regard for truth, correctness, morality, propriety, justice or appropriateness, one could find one's self pulling in a dragnet of undesirable and unprofitable types of rights. And since the notion is that everyone should be treated equal under the law, nobody's request should be denied; it is unconditional freedom. This means that the law must accommodate even that which is contrary to itself. The effort to combat this unmitigated liberation is the very reason why God instituted His moral and ethical codes in His written word via the Holy Bible.

That is why freedom cannot be absolute or limitless autonomy. A good example is a man who believes he is free to walk anywhere. Thus, he walks through a forested area, gets to the edge of a cliff and decides that he is free to walk off the cliff since it is his right to do so. Everyone knows the inevitable result. Need I say more?

Biblical Caution

The Apostle Peter cautions us in 1 Peter 2:16: "As free, yet not using liberty as a cloak for vice, but as bondservants of God." The Apostle Paul reinforces the point in 1 Corinthians 6:12:

> All things are lawful unto me, but all things are not expedient: all things are lawful for me, but I will not be brought under the power of any (KJV).

The New International Version of the Bible (NIV) puts it this way:

> "I have the right to do anything," you say—but not everything is beneficial. "I have the right to do anything"—but I will not be mastered by anything.

In other words, I am free to do anything I want, but that very thing can bring me into bondage, making me a slave to it. That is the big mistake that the majority of people are making. Freedom must be exercised within the context of that which is fitting and proper, ethical and moral, contributing to the dignity of the human person and within the ambit of the righteousness of God. Or else, we are heading for complete anarchy and absolute lawlessness as a human society.

Put another way, we can so overkill our freedom through manipulation of the law that the law becomes a fool to itself, creating its own monster that will not be tamed. Ironically, that is where the misconstruing of "equal rights" is taking the law in our day, where morality and ethics are seen as too archaic to be monitoring agents for that which is now widely regarded as acceptable practice. Thus, previously undesirable beliefs and practices are now being seen as the norm, despite their detrimental effects on morality and the integrity of the human race.

Is the Gender Crisis Imposed?

The present gender crisis does not appear to be linked to natural or scientific tenets or criteria, but rather generated by a kind of suppositional theory in which a position is taken concerning the signification of terminologies, without any empirical evidence to confirm such. The advocates of change on the gender landscape have majored on assumptions that they have now skilfully orchestrated into presuppositions, rendering their contrived findings as unquestionable in the circumstances. There is no doubt in this writer's view that this gender crisis is imposed on populations around the world by the power brokers of our day. It is real but unnatural.

2

DEMYSTIFYING SEX AND GENDER

Sex and gender are so emotionally rooted and shrouded in mystery that the average person seems to be mesmerized by mere reference to them. Most people do not have a clue as to the origin of these expressions and what they actually meant. Thus, many tend to be confused and completely enthralled by the spin that present-day intellectuals have put on these words. There is much too much unwarranted hype surrounding sex and gender, especially the latter, within recent times.

According to the Online Etymology Dictionary, the terminology "sex" is much more recent than most of us think. It first appeared in the 14th century, meaning "males or females collectively," and is derived from the Latin *sexus* (*a sex, state of being either male or female, gender*). It is often linked to the Latin *seco*, meaning to divide or cut, implying one section of the human race in contrast to the other. According to this source, sex meaning "quality of being male or female" was first recorded in the 1520s.[1]

As far as gender is concerned, the Online Etymology Dictionary reveals that the word gender as applied to male and

---
[1] Online Etymology Dictionary, s.v. sex

female became established between the 15th and 20th century. It is derived from the Old French expression gendre or genre, meaning "kind, species; character…"; also from the Latin genus meaning "race, stock, family; kind, rank, order; species… also '(male or female) sex.'"[2] This same dictionary makes a salient point: "gender came to be the usual English word for 'sex of a human being.'"[3]

Thus, originally, the word gender was used clearly to distinguish the two human sexes, male or female, making gender and sex essentially synonymous. There was no need to identify any other gender but male or female, or masculine or feminine. The use of the word gender was never intended to mean anything other than one or the other of the human sexes and its associated attitudes, behaviours, roles and functions as male or female, men or women and boys or girls.

The science of biology affirms that there are only two human sexes—male and female. Correspondingly, there are two genders linked to the biological and behavioural differences between male and female. The English Oxford dictionary defines sex as *"either of the two main categories (male and female) into which humans and most other living things are divided on the basis of their reproductive functions."*[4] The World Health Organization (W.H.O) points out: *"Sex refers to the biological characteristics that define humans as female or male."*[5] The Miriam Webster's definition of gender is simply *"sex,"* or *"the behavioral, cultural, or psychological traits typically associated with one sex."* [6]

Further, it should be noted that at the time of the introduction of the terminologies "sex" and "gender" to the male/female dichotomy there was no change in the nature of relationship, behaviour, attitude, social norms or any other particularities

---

[2] Ibid, s.v. gender
[3] Ibid.
[4] English Oxford Dictionary, s.v. sex
[5] The World Health Organization, "Sexual and Reproductive Health," https://www.who.int/reproductivehealth/topics/sexual_health/sh_definitions/en/
[6] Miriam Webster s.v. gender

between the sexes. The reason is that these words, when introduced, were just new lingos or phraseologies to designate the two different divisions, sections, kinds or species of the human race that had been in existence from the creation of man (Gen. 1:27), some six thousand years before by the biblical account. Put another way, the behavioural and attitudinal characteristics or the established roles and functions of men as opposed to women, or boys as opposed to girls, were already in their proper perspectives, eons before the introduction of the terms sex or gender.

So that the new words sex and gender, when introduced, neither added nor took away from the significance of human male/female relationship or behaviour. From time immemorial there were male and female human beings, masculine and feminine, set apart mainly for the purpose of procreation or the perpetuating of the human race. This is the very reason why you and I are in existence in the 21st century, and this is the means by which our posterity will be begotten as well. The biblical account in Genesis 1:26-28 attests to this. Of course, sexual pleasure is a fringe benefit, but by no means the main purpose.

How then can such recent nomenclature like sex and gender, introduced simply to distinguish between the male and female human species, be now made to create such furore and pandemonium within human society? What accounts for the sudden change in the meaning of gender? Did some brilliant mind suddenly discover some profound nuance of the word? What exactly is the rationale for regarding gender as no longer pegged to or representing sex? Who created the rights for anybody to make gender mean anything other than sex and its associated attitudes, behaviours, roles and functions within human society? What makes gender so important and different now that it must be disconnected from sex and be considered a social construct, rather than linked to human biology?

A Circular Argument

Moreover, what is the rationale for one to claim now that human gender encompasses a whole range of types, when the word originally applied to an already existing male/female dichotomy that had always been the norm in human society? Are the advocates of such changes attempting to dispel over 6000 years of human sexual history with a speculative, suppositional theory which has no empirical or scientific evidence by which it is supported? The irony of this incredulous claim is that although gender is removed from a sex base and regarded as a social construct, yet, in reality, it superimposes itself on and alters human sexuality in an unprecedented and incredible manner.

It should be noted that every practical application of a so-called gender type demands a particular change in sexual behaviour. Put another way, although same sex advocates claim that gender is not based on sex, there is a different sexual tag that appears every time a gender type is practiced. In other words, the attempt to separate gender from sex in terms of meaning simply culminates in a logical fallacy called circular reasoning, in which the premises do not support the conclusion.[7] That is, it is impossible to separate gender from sex; everywhere gender goes, sex is inevitably there. How crafty and cunning could the human intellect be, yet not wise enough to recognize this grave error in attempting to separate gender from sex! Once the premise is wrong, every argument based on it is fallacious, in spite of how scholarly presented. The ridiculous result of this is that sex is forced to be a "social construct," an impossible result, even by same sex advocate standards. In reality, gender and sex are synonymous.

Power-broking Societal Changes on Baseless Premises

As a social construct, the new-found gender liberality is being used to remove original or natural sexual boundaries, which is proving to be detrimental to the existence of the natural

---
[7] Encyclopedia Britannica, s.v. Circular argument

family of one father, one mother and children. This has changed the value system designed to develop the personality of our young, impressionable minds, in particular. Young children are increasingly becoming undisciplined, frustrated, out of control and suicidal. Natural law and order are being ignored and superseded by the quest for personal aggrandizement and the satisfaction of strange or queer human feelings. Where is human society heading if not to utter chaos and anarchy with this unwarranted overemphasis and disproportionate application of gender?

In reality, and by reason of its origin, gender could never be superior to sex as a determinant of human sexual behaviour; it is merely equivalent to it, just as the etymological findings indicate. Moreover, it was never intended to be different from sex. Is there a hidden agenda here? In fact, can a semblance of plagiarism be ruled out here, since, in reality, they have taken a word which was merely an expression denoting an existing, historical reality of the male/female dichotomy, and are now causing it to mushroom into a virtual sea of "gender" types? Doesn't this resemble intellectual imposition, to say the least, or some kind of social power play? Are we dealing with "power ethics" here, where those who are powerful in the society could simply make their own rules or come up with their own definitions, blatantly disregarding the laws of nature in the process, and any other objecting or objective voice?

Latest Scientific Findings

The spuriousness of the claim that homosexuality or sexual orientation is linked to a sexual genome has been confirmed in the latest scientific research work in which a colossal sample of over 477,000 participants was used. In the process, scientists painstakingly examined enormous "genome data banks, including that of 23andMe and the UK Biobank."[8] The conclusion

---
[8] Sara Reardon, "Massive Study Finds No Single Genetic Cause of Same-Sex Sexual Behavior," Scientific American, August 29, 2019. https://www.scientificamerican.com/article/massive-study-finds-no-single-genetic-

is that there was no single gene or group of genes that establish homosexual behaviour, whether it is gay, lesbian or any other sexual choice based on gender fluidity or other phenomenon.[9] Thus the notion that homosexuals are "born that way" cannot be substantiated scientifically.

What this means is that the cause of the foregoing is basically a matter of choice, and not biological drivers. Therefore, one is left with a world of speculation when it comes to advocating and enforcing societal changes on the basis of sexual orientation, homosexual thoughts or practice. Governments around the world, therefore, cannot blindly institute changes in family forms, sexual laws and general lifestyle options of its people simply on the basis of sexual orientation, and yet consider these under the "legitimacy" of human rights. The grounds for such alterations are unjustified scientifically and insufficient to warrant any imposition whatsoever. Human rights are naturally accruing and are not based merely on personal choices; if that were so, nobody should be judged to be in error legally or otherwise when he or she makes a personal choice—be it murder, violence, embezzlement, burglary or the like.

---

cause-of-same-sex-sexual-behavior/
[9] Ibid.

3

THE CREATION ACCOUNT

Let us carefully examine the original plan of God:

> And the earth was without form, and void; and darkness was upon the face of the deep. And the Spirit of God moved upon the face of the waters. And God said, Let there be light: and there was light (Gen. 1:1-3)

In order for us to comprehend fully God's creative order, and to fathom the decree to which post-modern thinkers have diverted from the Creator's master design, we are constrained to carefully examine the Biblical account. According to Genesis chapter 1, *"in the beginning,"* the earth was without form and it was empty; darkness was *"upon the face of the deep"* (v. 2). God then initiated created life in the earth by the Spirit of God moving (Heb. *merathepet*), that is fluttering over the waters as an eagle would flutter over her nest. It seems reasonable to speculate that that agitated motion could have been the means by which God was generating the foundation elements for the various life forms that He was about to create.[10]

The biblical account is fundamentally scientific. The first thing that God spoke into being was light: "'Let there be light'; and there was light." We are all aware of the necessity for light energy as an essential ingredient in sustaining life in the earth. Thus, as a key provision for supporting or upholding subsequent life forms, God called light into being. The Bible says that Jesus is the light of the world (Jn. 8:12). All three persons of the Godhead were involved in the Act of creation. God the Father superintended the whole process; the Holy Spirit oscillated over the waters and the Son (Jesus) came forth as light and laid the foundation for all living creatures that were to be generated through creation. John the apostle wrote of Jesus: "In Him was life, and the life was the light of men" (Jn. 1:4).

God afterwards established day and night by dividing the light from the darkness (Gen. 1:4-5). This was followed by the calling into being of a firmament to separate the waters above from the waters below the firmament (vv. 6-7). He then formed the seas by gathering the waters that were under the heavens into one place, causing dry land (earth) to appear (vv. 9-10).

God then spoke to the earth that it should bring forth grass, seed-yielding herbs, and fruit-yielding trees after their kind; and it was so. The evening and the morning were the third day. God thereafter spoke into being bodies of lights into the firmament of the heavens, *"to divide the day from the night"*; and that they would be "for signs and seasons, for days and years." Among these lights were two great lights –"the greater light to rule the day" (the sun), "and the lesser light to rule the night" (the moon). This was the fourth day (vv. 12-19).

God then spoke to the waters that they should abound with living creatures, including birds that would fly *"above the earth across the face of the firmament of the heavens."* Great sea

---

[10] Pastor Lisa Singh, teaching in an annual conference, Divine Partakers New England Apostolic Prophetic Conference, April 2016, Divine Encounter Fellowship, Trinidad, W.I.

creatures and every moving creature abounded in the waters; God blessed them and set them to multiply and fill the waters of the sea; and set birds to multiply on the earth. This was the fifth day (Gen. 1:20-23). Pay careful attention to where the birds came from—from the waters. This is interesting, and some food for thought for the evolutionist, in that birds carry some type of primordial scales on their legs and feet as well as a spread of wings equivalent to the fins of fish. Do you see the similarity in action of fish swimming and gliding through the ocean with birds flying through the firmament of air above? Don't birds come after fish in the evolutionary chain? How scientific is the Bible?

On the sixth and last day of creation, God spoke to the earth that it should bring forth the living creatures after their kind, such as cattle, beast and creeping creatures after their kind. Pay attention to the phenomenon of God so far calling all His creation into existence; this is in contrast to what He was to do next in the process of creation.

God's Masterpiece:
A Creature after His Own Image and Likeness

God then embarked on a master plan as He set out to produce His highest order of creation—man. God acts here like the Chief Executive Officer of a great enterprise, complete with design layout as well as vision and mission statements. His vision for man is outlined in verse 26 of Genesis chapter 1:

> Let us make man in our image, according to our likeness; let them have dominion over the fish of the sea, over the birds of the air, and over the cattle, over all the earth and over every creeping thing that creeps on the earth.

He would make a creature after His own image and likeness, who would share in His dominion and rule over His earthly creation.

Let us explore the perception of God making man after His

own image and likeness. Whereas He called the other living creatures into being, the Scripture reveals in Genesis 2:7, that God formed man from the red dust of the earth; then breathed into his nostrils the breath (Heb. *nishmat*) of life. This Hebrew word translates as "strong wind, blast or inspiration." In other words, God released His life into the human race quite forcibly, not merely by way of a gentle puff of air. Another related word in the Hebrew is *ruach* which means wind (Exod. 10:13), breath (Gen. 7:15) or spirit (Eccl. 12:7). I believe that *nishmat* is used in Genesis 2:7 to signify the power of the initial transfer of the breath of life into the otherwise lifeless human body, signifying a once and for all release of human life, which then spread from Adam to all human offspring.

The essential nature of God is "spirit" as revealed in John 4:24: "God is Spirit, and those who worship Him must worship in spirit and truth." The Greek equivalent for spirit is "pneuma." If God made us in His own image and likeness, then God made us essentially spirit beings, meaning that our earthly bodies are merely conveyors of the real "you" or "me." When God formed man from the dust of the ground and breathed into his nostrils the breath of life, God gave man part of Himself. Thus, what we call the human spirit is not human in nature, that is, originating from the humus of the earth, but divine. It is only regarded as the "human spirit" by virtue of its association with a human being.

Designed to Fulfil Purpose

Now one man could not take dominion over God's vast creation. Thus, God had to put a design in place to multiply the species so that there would be many human beings spread over the earth to carry out God's mandate. That is the reason why in verse 27, the Scripture says:

> So God created man in His own image; in the image of God He created him; male and female He created them.

The word for male in the Hebrew is *zakar,* which according

to the Brown, Driver and Briggs Hebrew-English Lexicon is dual in meaning—"sharp male organ" (phallus or penis) and "competence to worship." The word for female is *nekevah* which means "pierced" or "womb or opening," fittingly complimenting *zakar* for the purpose intended—to be fruitful, multiply and subdue the earth (that is, procreation).[11] God made it clear from the beginning that there would be a visible, outward and undeniable evidence of maleness or femaleness (i.e., the difference in the genitalia). He made them sexually distinctive from the outset.

One did not have to be schooled in rocket science to distinguish male from female. One could have easily made the distinction by sight; this is a reflection of the wisdom of our Creator. That is why the doctor could say at birth, "You have a boy!" or, "You have a girl!" Anyone could tell. Further, the male's anatomy matures differently to the female's. The man develops a more rugged physique, with bones and muscles much tougher in feel and appearance. His voice goes through a change from light-pitched and mild to increasingly deeper and stronger, as he enters puberty. He also typically develops facial hairs, and eventually a beard, wherever he allows the facial hairs to proliferate. The root of all this is both hormonal and genetic, as I would explain in the next chapter.

On the other hand, our Creator endowed the female with the appropriate amenities to ensure the development of more supple muscle tone, and a lighter and milder voice pitch, among other things. She is also built differently in the hip region to accommodate pregnancy. As a result, she walks differently to the man. She is also outfitted with a uterus so as to allow for conception, incubation, development and conveyance of the young foetus to the point of delivery. Moreover, she develops a pair of mammary glands as she enters into puberty, for the main purpose of postnatal care. This is not incidental; it is by divine design.

---

[11] Francis Brown, S.R. Driver, Charles A. Briggs, Hebrew and English Lexicon of the Old Testament, s.v. zakar and nekevah.

There was no need for the male to be endowed as the female since his function was different. It has always been clear that the male (*zakar*) human body could never conceive; he was not designed for that. His body is structured to facilitate, among other things, the release of the male "seed" of reproduction (the sperm) into the woman for the act of procreation. Correspondingly, the female (*nekevah*) body is structured to receive the male genital and sperms; the science of biology shows that the very muscles in the vagina are inward contracting so as to naturally accommodate the act of coitus.

Design is linked to Purpose

Once the design was in place, God then spelled out His mission statement for man:

> Be fruitful and multiply; fill the earth and subdue it; have dominion over the fish of the sea, over the birds of the air, and over every living thing that moves on the earth (Gen. 1:28).

Thus, God delivered the creation mandate (man's mission) to our first parents—to be fruitful, multiply, subdue and take dominion over the earth.

It is a truism that design is linked to purpose. The design of a thing indicates its intended use. For example, an aeroplane is designed to fly; it would be utterly foolish to attempt to drive down the highway with an aeroplane just because it has an engine and wheels. To do so would be foolish and self-destructive; it should not be done, it ought not to be attempted. In simple language, one would be misusing or abusing the airplane, resulting in grave consequences. In the same token, one cannot use a motorcar to fly; it was not designed for that. The fatalism of that act need not be reiterated. Neither can you pull a boat from the waters and believe that because it is running so smoothly on the waters, covering so many knots per hour that it would do well on the road. It is inappropriate and unwise for one to simply ignore the design of something and use it for whatever purpose one wishes.

As we hinted earlier, the male man (*zakar*) is structured to be a giver or supplier of seed; it is rather asinine to consider a man receiving seed from a woman, far less from another man. In the design of our Creator, there is no natural portal for a man to receive seed. Science affirms that the muscular contraction of the anus (comprised of the internal and external anal sphincter muscles) is directed outward for the purpose of elimination of faecal matter and gas, since it marks the end of the gastrointestinal tract. In other words, nature speaks its own language here. Those who dare to ignore nature can only do so at their own peril.

So, why did God make us male and female from the beginning? The answer is clearly to facilitate the multiplication of the human race, since one male man could not rule over God's vast creation; neither can he duplicate himself (self-propagate) in order to do so. The male/female duality was not an accident. None of us would be here had God not purposely designed us male and female. Thus one cannot just arbitrarily equalize the sexes regardless of the genitalia that someone possesses. That's bordering on insanity. Thus, from the standpoint of the biblical account and nature itself, there is no hint that gender is significantly different to sex since the only basic division of the human race to consider is male and female.

4

NATURE'S EVIDENCE OF GOD'S CREATIVE MANDATE

Internal Male/Female Distinctions

With the advancement in science, internal distinctions between male and female have been clearly established. The first crucial internal distinction lies in the area of genetics—the chromosomal content of the cells. The normal human cell is characterized by 23 pairs of chromosomes, the last pair being the determiner of human sex—sex chromosomes—XY in males and XX in females. That is why the male determines the sex of the offspring and not the female. That is, in the process of human reproduction (requiring the splitting and copulation of cells), the male can provide either X chromosomes or Y chromosomes; the female can only contribute X chromosomes.

In the wisdom of our Creator, the reproductive cells—the sperm in the males and the ovum (egg) in the females—carry only half the number of chromosomes. At conception, the full contingent of 23 pairs of chromosomes is re-established in the developing zygote, already bearing the genetic stamp of either male or female. The offspring, therefore, is already either a girl or boy, long before the physical distinctions are seen in the various trimesters of the developing foetus. Again, none of this is incidental or accidental. This is by Divine order. This happens consistently despite some anomalous genetic accidents here and there.

Now, it is the opinion of this writer that because of sin and the fall of man, there were detrimental effects on the whole human person, not only his spiritual condition. The Bible points out that the wages of sin is death (Rom. 6:23), and that through one man's (Adam's) sin, sin entered into the human race and death through sin (Rom. 5:12ff). If sin resulted in death, then it stands to reason that sin could have also disrupted certain genetic pathways and, in the odd case, negatively influence the perfect order of human reproduction, resulting in occasional genetic mutations or accidents.

The foregoing should explain why some medical experts point out that some people may carry XXY or XYY chromosomes and the like, as the case may be, or in some cases, undeveloped or over developed genitals. But these are the exceptions rather than the rule. This is a matter for medical science and no justification for designating a spectrum of genders. For similar reasons, the odd person is born with undeveloped body parts such as hands, legs, toes, eyes, internal organs, you name it. Such people understand that life may not be as congenial as if they had their full contingent of standard body parts. Thus, they know that their condition is exceptional and not the norm. So that classifying a person as a new gender merely on the basis of genetic mutations (which are no more than anomalies of normal genetic transfers) is unwarranted.

The second major internal difference between the human male and female has to do with their hormonal construct. In the woman, a group of hormones known as estrogens (sex hormones) has the overwhelming influence. They include estrone, estradiol and estriol and are responsible for female features such as breasts, wider hips, regulation of the menstrual cycle and the like; there is also a small amount of testosterone. Estrogen works with another hormone, progesterone, to promote and maintain pregnancy, including fertilization, implantation, and nutrition of the early embryo. There is a large range of other benefits of estrogens in the female body.[12]

On the other hand, the male man is distinguished by the predominance of androgens, comprised mostly of testosterone and other male hormones with a small amount of estrogen (female hormone). Testosterone promotes sex drive, male fertility, bone mass, muscle size and strength and other distinct male features. Sometimes there may be a higher than normal proportion of testosterone in females which may cause some male features to develop[13] but again, this is the exception rather than the rule.

In light of the foregoing facts, the male/female duplicity in human beings is hardly arbitrary or whimsical so that one could simply "name" one's self a male or female regardless of whatever genitalia one carries, or whatever one's genotype or hormonal composition. Our Creator made sure that male and female indicators were evident both outwardly and internally, so that there would be no gender confusion as our world seems to be embroiled in at this time of human history. Indeed, what our Creator designed Himself could not be incidental or even accidental. It is His personal vision, objectivity, plan and purpose for man.

The Intricacies of Pregnancy Demonstrate God's Creative Order

The mystery of pregnancy itself testifies to the special endowment of our Creator on womanhood. The evidence cannot be glided over and treated as incidental to human life. The first stage of pregnancy is fertilization in which one

---

[12] Onlymyhealth. Process of Construction to Birth. https://www.onlymyhealth.com/process-conception-birth-1345140048 and other internet sources.
[13] Ibid.

of the 400 million to 500 million sperms released through male ejaculation swims up the Fallopian tube and eventually reaches and fertilizes the one egg or ovum released by the woman.

The result is conception, in which the sex and all other determinate features of the new person are immediately set in the zygote formed.[14] The next stage is implantation. Just after fertilization, the zygote develops into the embryo which is in essence a "distinct individual." The woman's menstrual cycle discontinues because of the hormonal changes and signals of pregnancy triggered off in the reproductive system. Pregnancy normally lasts for 38-40 weeks (approximately nine (9) months) from the day of conception.[15]

After implantation, a protective fluid-filled capsule, the amniotic sac, develops around the embryo. A separate organ called the placenta then develops, connecting the developing foetus to the uterine wall to allow nutrient and oxygen intake and waste elimination from the baby's body. The umbilical cord then develops and connects the embryo to the placenta. The latter acts like a surrogate "mother" in the womb, transferring materials to and fro the mother's blood without allowing direct mixing of the mother's blood with the child's.[16]

By the end of the first month of pregnancy, internal organs like kidneys, heart and liver begin to form. By the second month, the brain has begun to develop. By the third month facial features, dental buds and limbs are already showing, while cartilage begins to turn into bones establishing a foetus.[17]

By the third month, the baby's arms, fingers, feet and toes are seen as well as the beginnings of fingernails, toenails, and

---

[14] Ibid.
[15] Ibid.
[16] Wikipedia, s.v. umbilical cord. https://en.wikipedia.org/wiki/Umbilical_cord
[17] "Fetal Development Stages of Growth," Cleveland Clinic blog. https://my.clevelandclinic.org/health/articles/7247-fetal-development-stages-of-growth.

teeth. "By the end of the third month, your baby is fully formed."[18] By the beginning of the second trimester, research has shown that the baby is listening. By the fifth to the sixth month, the sex or gender of the baby can be identified by the doctor through ultrasound. Movement begins to be evident in the baby as he or she responds to external and internal sounds. One could see the baby's eyebrows forming. The baby also changes position as it swims around in the amniotic fluid. By the seventh to eight month, the mother begins to feel kicks from her baby. The foetus could react to light and listen to voices from outside. Thus a mother can talk to her baby at this time and begin to bond with her offspring even before birth. The foetus begins to get ready for birth; its bone marrow and red blood corpuscles are being fully established.[19]

By the ninth month, the baby is then ready for delivery. Normally, at delivery, strong, regular contractions begin; the mother goes into labour as the water bag breaks and the baby emerges, head-first. The sight and the cry of the baby, plus being able to hold the young treasure, far outweigh the pain and trauma endured by the mother in child bearing.[20]

How can anyone conclude that the foregoing is all by chance? Are the complexities and the amazing intricacies of female pregnancy to be simply glided over as an either/or occurrence? Can a male man ever do the same? Is this not the work and design of a Master Creator? Then from where do same-sex union advocates get their warrant, disregarding God's creation order and inventing their own notion of equality? Who on earth would dare interfere with the intricacies of the Master's workmanship? Are we seeing an uncanny or ghoulish attempt to replace God here?

---

[18] Ibid.
[19] Ibid.
[20] Ibid.

Equality of Value Not Equality of Function

How could one claim equality of the sexes on a carte blanche basis, when there is so much scientific and pragmatic evidence to show clear distinction of roles and functions between a man and a woman? The problem with same-sex advocates' notion of equality is that a clear demarcation is not being made between equality in value and equality in function. Can one honestly look at the female anatomy, hormonal content, genetic distinctions, combined with the intricacies of female pregnancy and still claim equality in function and role between male and female? Like I pointed out before, the role and function of a woman as distinct from a man is properly established by our Creator designing us as He did for a specific purpose.

Equality in value between male and female is a truism that God Himself established from the beginning. If we go back to the Genesis account in Genesis chapter 2, we would see something that many have missed:

> [7]And the Lord God formed man of the dust of the ground, and breathed into his nostrils the breath of life; and man became a living being. [8]The Lord God planted a garden eastward in Eden, and there He put the man whom He had formed... [20] So Adam gave names to all cattle, to the birds of the air, and to every beast of the field. But for Adam there was not found a helper comparable to him. [21] And the Lord God caused a deep sleep to fall on Adam, and he slept; and He took one of his ribs, and closed up the flesh in its place. [22] Then the rib which the Lord God had taken from man He made into a woman, and He brought her to the man.

Notice that God formed the man, gave him responsibility or work to dress the garden and keep it, and also gave him the task of naming the animals. Thus, the man was clearly established by God to be the leader with assigned duties before the woman came. God, in doing so, demonstrated the nobility and dignity of work. All this took place before sin and the fall of man came into the equation. It was only after Adam sinned that God cursed the ground that he tilled and decreed that by the sweat of his face (by much toil) he would eat bread (Gen. 3:17). In other words, work would become a burden for him.

It was intriguing that although Adam was moving around as a male man, not generic man, that the woman was tucked away in the form of a special bone in the ribcage. We know that from the fact that God, in seeking to make for Adam a "help meet," simply put the man into a deep sleep (the first anaesthetic) and extracted a rib from him and closed back the flesh thereof (the first surgery).[21] This rib He then developed into a full-blown functional woman. That should not be difficult to understand since the bone carries the bone marrow, the source of red blood cells, white blood cells and platelets. When one considers that the life of the flesh is in the blood (Leviticus 17:11), one is sure that Eve was not an unrealistic invention, but was simply made into a fully functional woman from the rib of the man when God was ready to do so.

The point must be reiterated that when God formed Adam Eve was also part of that design, demonstrating that they were both equal in terms of value in God's eyes. She was not an afterthought. Based on the vision, design, mission and the ultimate purpose for making man, Eve could never have been incidental. She was always part of the initial conception of thought and the final blueprint of God for His making us in His own image and likeness to have dominion over the earth. As mentioned earlier, God knew that one man could not take care of His vast creation. He had to make them male and female.

Why then did God not make the two individuals functional at the same time? There might have been several reasons for this:

I. *He wanted to establish their distinct functional positions.*
God made it absolutely clear who was to be the leader of

---
[21] Genesis 2:18-22

the family by making the man functional first and giving him responsibility. If God had made them both functional at the same time and placed them side by side in the Garden, there would have been a jostling for leadership, since neither of them could tell who was the leader.

II. *To allow the man to yearn for a companion.* Having been given the mandate to be fruitful and multiply and realizing that he could not do so by himself, God expected Adam to add value to the one that would complement him in fulfilling his God-ordained purpose. Consequently, she would be honoured in his sight.

III. *By hiding Eve in the ribcage of Adam, he would regard her as hidden treasure and add worth to her.* When Adam finally saw her, he exclaimed: "This is now bone of my bone and flesh of my flesh; she shall be called woman because she was taken out of man" (Gen. 2:23).

IV. *To avoid confusion in roles.* That is, Eve would come and meet Adam already working and would understand that she is to be helper (not as an inferior servant or slave, but as an invaluable facilitator) of Adam's cause. One of the major things she would do is to exploit Adam's potential to perpetuate seed and in the process make him fruitful. She would act as comforter and vital support to Adam to allow the human race to forge ahead in fulfilling God's creation mandate.

V. *To illustrate that the man should be the covering for the woman at all times.* By the law of first mention, the woman having been first placed in the ribcage of the man means that she should be always covered by the man. Even when she was taken out of man and developed into a fully functional woman, God brought her back to the man and entrusted her into his hands, no doubt implying that he was now responsible for taking care of her. God acted as father of the bride, who was passing on the responsibility for covering, back to the man Adam, no doubt implying that she was always covered and protected by him and that he should resume his responsibility, albeit she was now fully functional and outside of the ribcage.

Equality of value is extremely clear and very logical based on God's own design. But equality of role and function between the sexes is unreal and groundless, downright illogical. The differences in the anatomy, the DNA and the hormones between a man and a woman naturally reflect completely different roles and functions. Any deviation from what is dictated by nature and by God's creation mandate would have to be viewed as imposed, forced and unnatural.

This writer wishes to reiterate that the woman was not an after-thought of God. She was already conceived in God's heart when He was forming the man. This makes her equal to the man, not in form or design, but in value. However, they enjoy two different functional positions that when viewed collectively are equally essential to the purpose intended by our Creator. So that, although equal in value, their functions are distinct. The man was established as leader by virtue of being made functional first and is clearly the donor of seed while the woman was created as a help meet for her husband as afore mentioned.

Nekevah (Female): Designed to Be Equal

A closer look at the expression "help meet" as seen in the King James Version (KJV) of the Bible (Gen. 2:18) would reveal a whole lot about God's intention for making the woman equal in value to her male counterpart. The original Hebrew rendering is *ezer kenegdo*. We will first look at various translations of that expression in different versions of the Bible, then look more closely at the Hebrew text itself.

KJV: "And the LORD God said, It is not good that the man should be alone; I will make him an help meet for him." One who will help him meet his needs; fulfill his desires

NKJV: And the Lord God said, "It is not good that man should be alone; I will make him a helper comparable to him." As compared to the other creatures.

NIV: The Lord God said, "It is not good for the man to be alone. I will make a helper suitable for him." A helper providing just what he needs

RIV: Then the Lord God said, "It is not good that the man should be alone; I will make him a helper fit for him." Helping to meet his expectations and satisfy him.

Let us now examine the original *ezer kenegdo* and see the profound wisdom of God in demonstration. On the surface, the expression "help meet" seems to place emphasis on the woman satisfying the needs of the man. If one is not careful, one could easily misinterpret the expression to suggest that God set up the man as an egotistic male chauvinist, who by his very existence puts a demand on the wife to satisfy him, meet his needs and fulfil his desires or else! A proper word study of *ezer kenegdo* will eliminate that impression.

The first word in the expression in the phrase is *ezer which* means "helper." The second word *ke**negd**o* is comprised of a root word *neged*, a prefix "*ke*" and a suffix "*o*". The prefix "*ke*" means "like," and the suffix "*o*" means "of him" or "of his." Therefore, just with the prefix and the suffix alone one gets "a helper ... like him." Thus one could easily say that God provided for man a helper like him.

Before we look further at *kenegdo*, it is necessary to examine *ezer* a little deeper. In the context of Genesis 1:18, it does not mean what the average person thinks. According to Marg Mowczko, *ezer* refers to superior help, such as "the assistance provided by doctors." She argues that the word *ezer* "is always and only used in the OT in the context of vitally important and powerful acts of rescue and support."[22] Of the twenty-one times the word is used in the OT, two times it is used in reference to Eve, three times with reference to people in general, but sixteen (16) times it is used to refer to God as "helper."[23] Two verses showing such use are:

> Ps. 70:5: "But I am poor and needy; make haste to me, O God! You are my help (ezer) and my deliverer; O Lord, do not delay"; and Psalm 121:2: "My help (ezer) comes from the Lord, who made heaven and earth.."

Thus, the word helper as it refers to the first woman must not be viewed as subservience in the face of her male counterpart. The word "help" or "helper" implies something very different in Hebrew than it does in English. Kat Armas asserts that in English "helper" invariably refers to a servant, apprentice or someone "under a person in authority." However, in Hebrew "help" suggests

> one who has *power* to give help—it refers to someone in a superior position offering help to a weaker person who cannot help herself or himself.[24]

In a sense, therefore, one can conclude that the woman as helper to the man brings to the relationship a power that is superior to what the latter possesses in specific areas. For example, her capacity to receive seed, conceive, incubate, carry, nourish and develop the young child, then release that offspring

---

[22] Marg Mowczko, "A Suitable Helper (in Hebrew." Exploring the biblical theology of Christian egalitarianism. Accessed June 28, 2019. https://margmowczko.com/a-suitable-helper.
[23] Ibid.
[24] Kat Armas, What Does "Helper" Really Mean? https://katarmas.com/blog/2018/8/3/what-does-helper-really-mean

into the world is unique to womanhood; not to mention that she then provides post-natal care and nourishment for her baby through her mammary paps. These and other intricate roles and functions put the woman to some degree in a league of her own, so to speak. The complementarity and equality of value between the man and the woman are glaring, to say the least. That is, the woman has the power to help the man in ways that he cannot help himself. *Zakar* needs *nekevah* in order to fulfil purpose and vice versa.

Now, we still have the root word *neged* to explore. This word carries several shades of meaning: "in front of, in sight of, opposite to, over against, corresponding to or other side."[25] Here is an intriguing finding: According to the Ancient Hebrew Research Centre, *neged*

> is always used in the causative form where it would literally be translated "to make to be face to face", and is always used to mean "to tell" in the sense of causing another to come face to face in order to tell them something.[26]

From the foregoing, one gets the picture of the woman being designed to be opposite to, over against, or to be on the other side of the man, face to face with him to converse with him, among other things.

Thus our translation so far should read:

> A helper like himself designed and positioned over against or face to face with

---

[25] Strong's Exhaustive Concordance of the Bible. #5048. Also Brown Driver and Briggs Hebrew English Lexicon, s.v. *neged*.
[26] Jeff A. Benner, "What is a "help meet?" Ancient Hebrew Research Center: Ploughing through History from the Aleph to the Tav.

him to provide for 'telling' him or discussing with him how things may be planned, organized and implemented going forward[27]

It is evident that dialogue was implied from the beginning and that the woman was to be a helper with similar yet opposite attributes to her male counterpart. It is interesting that Adam was not used to talking except to himself, since he did not have another human being with whom to converse. One could say that Eve (*nekevah*) came into Adam's life to initiate conversation. Is it any wonder then that women are very talkative while men tend to be more of the silent or reserved type?

This phenomenon of the woman being designed to be opposite to the man and complimentary to him, and their being both mutually equal in terms of value can be illustrated by considering the need for a human being to have a left hand and a right hand. Just imagine having two right hands instead of a left and a right. Or try shifting the right wing of an aeroplane to the left wing position; is this feasible? Nature itself demands opposites to ensure the workability of several processes. That is why in plumbing you have "male" and "female" fittings; and in electricity there are "male" and "female plugs. Which types are more important?." If one cannot dispense with such reality in everyday life, then what makes us feel that it is okay to ignore such reality in human society? It would be absurd to attempt to reconstruct a female plug to look the same as a male plug in order to enhance functionality?

Then why do some people believe that such a step is necessary in human society at this time? Are the tenets of so-called "advanced human existence" superior to the laws of nature?

---

[27] Author's version

5

THE DRIVING FORCE BEHIND GENDER CHANGE

The United States Agency for International Development (USAID) defines gender as:

> the array of socially constructed roles and relationships, personality traits, attitudes, behaviors, values, and relative power and influence that society ascribes to the two sexes on a differential basis. Gender is an acquired identity that is learned, changes over time, and varies widely within and across cultures. Gender is relational and refers not simply to women or men but to the relationship between them.[28]

The foregoing definition is alarming in the light of all we have discussed about gender so far. Gender was never meant

---

[28] USAID from the American people, "Gender Terminology" https://pdf.usaid.gov/pdf_docs/Pnadl089.pdf

to be a social construct if one looks carefully at its etymology. This writer reiterates that gender was first introduced simply as another aspect of the nomenclature for identifying the two sexes—male or female.

Who is the authority behind society ascribing sexual roles, relationships, behaviours, personality traits and other aspects of sexuality to individuals? What was the state of the male/female relationship before the introduction of the gender terminology? Was there some serious defect that "gender" would have removed? There was no evidence to this effect. Are we to discount the more than 6000 years of human relationship and sexual behaviour prior to this "grandiose new discovery" of gender? Moreover, where is the empirical evidence to prove that gender is *"an acquired identity"* learned over time and varying *widely within and across cultures*, referring *not simply to women or men but to the relationship between them*? Without such evidence this new concept of gender is merely speculative and detrimental to normal human relationship.

The foregoing redefinition of gender is a social sciences opinion, which, as we know, is largely philosophical or suppositional. How could such notions be used to alter male/female roles, functions, behaviours and the very demographics of society without scientific evidence? Is not this a serious digression from that place where postmodern society thinkers once prided themselves—in scientifically verified evidence? Were we not at one time quick to dismiss as unscientific any argument that did not satisfy empirical investigation? Then how has it become so easy to restructure society using speculative frameworks? Where are the biological or natural science findings for the strong advocacy exhibited by same-sex pundits?

Based on its etymology and its originally intended application, gender was meant to be a description of a fact of nature—that the human race is comprised of male and female only. A fact of nature cannot be redefined. This means that there was no room for gender as a social construct as it is now advocated by some.

For example, if one comes up with the novel idea of renaming the sun, would that change the reality of what the sun is or does, or vice versa? Would the sun still rise in the east and set in the west every day as it has been doing for time immemorial, or would it do so only seasonally? Likewise, a person's gender as male or female is a fact of nature that cannot change on the basis of notion or feelings. The social construct concept is mere speculation; and this is no basis for redefining something as fundamental as gender.

Yes, the only basis for seeing gender as a spectrum and not the natural phenomenon of male or female is to see it as a concept rather than a fact of nature. Who on earth has the authority to do so and then apply it to alter human sexual behaviour? Where and under what circumstances was the simple designation of gender as *gendre*, referring to the male or female species or kind, altered? What was the rationale for making the change? Was the original definition of the word faulty? Were there hidden ingredients in the word that the original users of the word missed? Or is there not now a misconstruing of the intended purpose of the word? Or, is there not a deliberate agenda to provide for the whims and fancies of unnatural sexual preferences, sexual orientation or personal or selfish pleasure?

Put another way, could the assumed "faultiness" of the original "gender" perspective be rooted in protest; that is, the unwillingness to acknowledge a clear distinctiveness between male and female gender? In this way, one would have less difficulty in the agenda of "equalizing" the sexes as the current wave of feminist movements and their emerging entities have been seeking to do? So then, was the original meaning of gender "faulty" from an objective or merely subjective standpoint? Is the new perspective on gender the experience of the majority of human beings or is it confined to a few people with an alleged or anecdotal notion?

The only way gender could be "faulty" in meaning is if it was originally intended to create greater enlightenment on the male/

female reality and in fact did not because of some oversight or human error. If that were so, then there would be justification to correct it now. But as we argued previously there is absolutely no hint of this in the etymology of the word. Thus, the present quest to redefine gender so that it is no longer pegged to sex is a subjective and contrived decision, concocted by minds that have a specific agenda.

Since we have no choice but to conclude that the idea of changing the meaning of gender is a subjective one, we cannot justify the complete overhauling of national or international laws (true law must be based on objective truth) to allow for the superimposing of unnatural practices on natural or standardized human sexual behaviour. On the one hand, the advocates for the redefinition of gender point out that gender is not to be confined by the two sexes and therefore should be defined independent of sex. On the other hand, although gender is now made out to be a spectrum of types independent of sex, ironically human sexual behaviour becomes engulfed by the very spectrum of gender types and fantasies, showing that the reasoning is fallacious, illogical and downright deceptive.

Differing Positions of World Authorities

The Beijing 1995 4th World Conference on Women

The position of "gender" as a social construct was officially established at the 4th World Conference on Women in Beijing 1995, when various definitions of the term 'gender' were proposed and ratified by the Beijing Platform for Action. Basically the following definition conveys the essence of the position held by the 1995 Beijing conference:

> Gender is used to refer to the social roles, responsibilities, behaviours, attitudes and identities as men and women which are the result of social, cultural and historical factors

as opposed to our biological differences.[29]

The first half of the foregoing definition rightly depicts the particularity of differences between male and female sexes or genders. The problem is the basis for the differences— *social, cultural and historical factors as opposed to biological differences.* Who is the authority in making this claim—the United Nations, world governments? Who has the power to make such fundamental and far-reaching decisions that would alter the very moral fabric of society? There must be a higher authority than man himself. Why is the basis for gender determination now shifting instead of being fixed to sex? Who gave the green light for it to now shift? Is there any organization on earth that can simply ignore the laws of nature and sanction acts contrary to nature merely on the basis of human opinion?

While the women of the United Nations (UN) and representatives of various governments around the world cannot be faulted for seeking the welfare of women and girls, who have suffered and are still suffering at the hands of their male counterparts, it appears that they have erred gravely in their approach to achieving equality. Included in the Beijing 1995 declarations were the following:

> Ensure the full implementation of the human rights of women and of the girl child as an inalienable, integral and indivisible part of all human rights and fundamental freedoms[30]

---

[29] Centre for Gender and Development Studies, University of the West Indies, May 20, 2004: Trinidad and Tobago Draft National Gender Policy and Action Plan, initiative of Ministry of Community Development, Culture and Gender Affairs, p. 3. In collaboration with the United Nations Development Programme and the CARICOM Gender Equality Programme, CIDA; the "Gender" definition adapted from concepts proposed and accepted at the 4th World Conference on Women in Beijing 1995.

[30] Declaration 9. http://www.un.org/womenwatch/daw/beijing/platform/declar.htm.

and

> Equal rights, opportunities and access to resources, equal sharing of responsibilities for the family by men and women, and a harmonious partnership between them are critical to their well-being and that of their families as well as to the consolidation of democracy[31]

On the surface, there seems to be nothing wrong with the foregoing aims. Notwithstanding, all of this could have been achieved without the need to redefine gender. Sound recommendations for implementing the above I am sure could have been made after carefully examining the social, cultural and historical reasons or causes for the gross inequalities meted out to women and girls by a male dominant society. There should have been no need to tamper with the laws of nature. Instead of seeking to change sexual codes to accommodate the quest for equality, the social scientists, practitioners, philosophers and other associated advocates of our day needed to pay more attention to causality and corrective action—prescriptive rather than descriptive ethics.

Here is another contrasting parallel for gender and sex used by the European Commission:

> Sex refers to the biologically determined differences between men and women, that are universal. Gender refers to social differences between women and men that are learned, changeable over time and have

---
[31] Ibid. Declaration 15.

wide variations both within and between cultures[32]

Again, where is the authority for the sharp line of demarcation between sex and gender? This differentiation is unwarranted. One cannot place a fact of nature like sex, which is scientifically attested to and universally true, on the same merit as a conceptual version of gender, suggesting that the latter is equally true and universal. The reasoning is spurious.

The Rome Statute of the International Criminal Court 1998

Three years after the Beijing conference, the International Criminal Court (ICC) found that the notion of "gender" as a "social construct," as established by the 4th World Conference on Women in Beijing 1995, was not workable in a Criminal court context. It could not satisfy the specificity required in criminal trials. Amidst heated debates and charges that the ICC definition was "stunningly narrow," "puzzling and bizarre," and resorting to "constructive ambiguity," among others,[33] the ICC insisted on the following definition of gender:

> For the purposes of this Statute, it is understood that the term 'gender' refers to the two sexes, male and female, within the context of society. The term 'gender' does not indicate any meaning different from the above.[34]

Valerie Oosterveld, in her comments on the Rome Statute

---

[32] A Guide to Gender Impact Assessment," European Commission. www.GuideToGender-IA.pdf

[33] Valerie Oosterveld, "The Definition of 'Gender' in the Rome Statute of the International Criminal Court: A Step Forward or Back for International Criminal Justice?" pp. 55-58. http://wikigender.org/wp-content/uploads/files/Definition_of_gender_in_the_Rome_Statute.pdf

[34] Ibid., p. 56.

of the International Criminal Court (ICC) 1998, reflects the suppositional nature of gender as viewed by the United Nations:

> While the definitions used and promoted within various parts of the U.N. differ in focus and wording, they all tend to emphasize three similar points: first, "gender" is a socially constructed concept; second, the construction of "gender" is complex and is influenced by culture, the roles women and men are expected to play, the relationships among those roles, and the value society places on those roles; and third, the content of "gender" can vary within and among cultures, and over time.[35]

In other words, gender, as redefined by same-sex advocates, is not decisive or conclusive and cannot, in this writer's perspective, carry the authority to allow it to superimpose itself over natural laws established by our Creator.

<u>The Holy See's Position</u>

Oosterveld noted that much support for the foregoing ICC definition of gender came from the Holy See which stated following the adoption of the Beijing accord:

> that it understood the term 'gender' "as grounded in biological sexual identity, male or female" and thus excluding "dubious interpretations based on world views which

---
[35] Ibid.

assert that sexual identity can be adapted indefinitely to suit new and different purposes[36]

The Rome Statute 1998 definition strongly implies, among other things, that when applied to real life situations requiring precise identity of individuals as required in criminal contexts, gender as a social construct was unworkable. That is, when put to the acid test, like in the case of medical science, social sciences' experiment on redefining gender as a social construct cannot withstand scrutiny. As was demonstrated before, the very etymology of the word affirms that there is no fundamental difference between sex and gender.

The World Health Organization

The World Health Organization (W.H.O.) claims the following:

'Gender' describes those characteristics of women and men that are largely socially created, while 'sex' encompasses those that are biologically determined. However, these terms are often mistakenly used interchangeably in scientific literature, health policy, and legislation.[37]

Again, the big question is how did bodies like the W.H.O determine the above, bearing in mind the etymology of the two words? How shocking and outrageous the claim that the terms sex and gender are "often mistakenly used interchangeably in scientific literature, health policy, and legislation," when in reality there is no empirical evidence to support the redefinition of gender! It should be the other way around—the W.H.O. and

---

[36] Ibid., p. 65
[37] World Health Organization; http://www.who.int/genomics/gender/en/

others appear to have now presumptuously misapplied the meaning of gender.

To claim that gender is "largely socially created" as opposed to sex which is "biologically determined" is a serious case of intellectual eisegesis. There is no justification for the claim. It seems clear that W.H.O.'s position is saturated with the framer's own presuppositions, biases, prejudices and agendas.

Dictionary Definitions

The Webster's Dictionary 1828 took into consideration the etymology of the word gender as rooted in the Latin "genus" meaning "kind" or " sort" and simply defines gender as "A sex, male or female."[38] The present-day Merriam-Webster gives a medical definition of gender as: "a : sex b: the behavioral, cultural, or emotional traits typically associated with one sex."[39] Here gender is synonymous with sex and the respective behavioural traits reflective of male or female sex.

Alarmingly, the following new definition of gender is now entrenched in the English Oxford Living Dictionaries:

> Either of the two sexes (male and female), especially when considered with reference to social and cultural differences rather than biological ones. The term is also used more broadly to denote a range of identities that do not correspond to established ideas of male and female.[40]

---

[38] Webster's Dictionary 1828—Online Edition. http://webstersdictionary1828.com/Dictionary/gender

[39] Merriam-Webster Word Central dictionary, s.v. sex, gender. http://wordcentral.com/cgi-bin/student?gender

[40] English Oxford Living Dictionaries. https://en.oxforddictionaries.com/definition/gender.

It is unfortunate that the social sciences bias has finally influenced our current dictionary definitions, despite the lack of justification for the change. This type of superfluous, unnatural reasoning is set to create utter confusion in the minds and emotions of the next generation, a fitting catalyst for disorientation and depression. Yet again, what are the grounds for distinguishing gender from sex on the basis of *social and cultural differences rather than biological ones"*? Was this ever hinted in the etymology of the word? Who has the moral supremacy to authorize or assign such a change?

The change in the meaning of gender cannot just be a simple case of option or opinion, considering that it is being used to alter human norms and established moral, ethical and spiritual values. How can it ever be right for one to import previously unrelated ideas to a word like gender and radically mutate its meaning, causing it to superimpose itself on natural human sexual behaviour and family life? That is nothing but high-level intellectual manipulation and dishonesty. The intellectuals of our day owe it to this generation to explain unambiguously the warrant or justification for the change in the meaning of gender.

This writer views this largely unfounded change as a case of "power ethics," in which those in society who hold the reins of power have deliberately ignored God's truth, and created their own "truth" and ground for right and wrong, virtually attempting to take the place of God. What they proclaim and have been enforcing in societies around the world are clearly spurious and untenable; yet they are using it to change moral and ethical values of human communities. How could this be allowed in a modern society that boasts of being so scientific and empirical about everything else? Is there an accommodation of convenience here? There seems to be a strong current of hypocrisy and presumptuousness if you ask me.

Gender, the Wrong Target for Achieving Sexual Equality

Ideally the home should be the target for change, and not "gender," since the home is the basic unit of society. As hinted above, world bodies like the U.N, W.H.O., P.A.H.O., UNICEF and others should focus their skills, expertise and funding on more effective programs to discover the real causes of dysfunctional homes and recommend more remedies in this regard. They should now provide more assistance to parents in training our young men especially to learn how to respect and see equal value in women in general. More special counselling, training and orientation sessions should be organized by family planning arms of governments to help would-be husbands to appreciate the women with whom they would be sharing life. Some kind of orientation program should also be developed for adult men, both married and unmarried, to help them recognize the true value of women.

Likewise, provisions should be made by world governing bodies to help orient women and girls to showing respect for the men in their lives. In the pursuit of "women's rights," many gender movements have engendered animosity and sarcasm against male leadership in the home and society at large. In the process, the inevitable approach has been to "get even." This passion has been translated into a "protest" approach, resulting in extreme and presumptuous measures being taken such as the one in question in this book—the redefinition of gender and the introduction of myriads of gender-types and an intensification of gender confusion.

In this mad rush to level the sexual/gender playing field, the outcome has been the removal of all lines of demarcation between male and female as our Creator originally established them. In other words, the corrective measures attempted have been artificial rather than natural, absurd rather than judicious. They are self-propelled instead of God-sanctioned, dangerous and destructive rather than contributing to societal development.

The biblical account shows that our Creator created us (male and female) [sex or gender]—equal. Each sex is designed to hold a different functional position that is as equally important as the other—father or mother, husband or wife. As argued earlier, the woman was never an afterthought of God; both male and female were conceived at the same time in God's blueprint for creating man. It was the fall of man and the resulting distortions that have been responsible for male chauvinism and unfair male domination throughout human history.

Any corrective action must be linked to: (i) the male man understanding who he is and discovering his true purpose and (ii) the woman knowing who she is and the role that she was designed by God to play. Ultimately it would require that God deal with man's heart (conscience), not man assuming the place of God and attempting to equalize the roles of male and female in an attempt to create a genderless society. I expand on this in the next chapter.

6

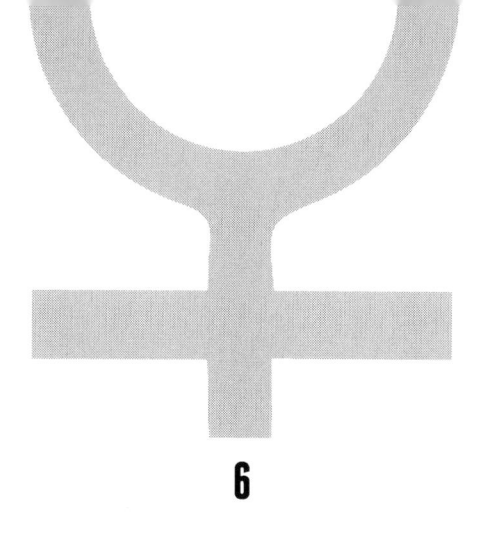

The Current Feminist Agenda vs. the Creation Account

Feminist ideology has been a major instigator in the kinds of changes now being made in sexual norms and behaviours in various cultures. According to Encyclopaedia Britannica, feminism is

> the belief in social, economic, and political equality of the sexes. Although largely originating in the West, feminism is manifested worldwide and is represented by various institutions committed to activity on behalf of women's rights and interests.[41]

Cambridge Dictionary defines feminism as:

> The belief that women should be allowed the same rights, power, and opportunities

---
[41] Encyclopaedia Britannica, s.v. *feminism*

as men and be treated in the same way, or the set of activities intended to achieve this state."[42]

This movement has gone through various waves of development, from the 19th and early 20th centuries (first wave), mid-20th century (late 60's to early 70's: 2nd wave), late 20th and early 21st centuries (particularly from early 90's: 3rd wave), plus other recent waves, stemming from a resurgence in 2012, centred on the social media.[43] Feminism ideology is marked by a sociological perspective as opposed to a biological one in treating with human sexuality and gender issues. They assert that gender is not biologically determined and "that gender differences result from cultural practices and social expectations that gender is socially constructed."[44]

Feminists generally hold that

...feminism is a commitment to achieving the equality of the sexes. This radical notion is not exclusive to women: men, while benefiting from being the dominant sex, also have stake in overcoming the restrictive roles that deprive them of full humanity.[45]

Here is where the water gets muddy, and the lines of demarcation of the sexes, sexual behaviour and roles are virtually

---

[42] Cambridge Dictionary, s.v. feminism
[43] M. A. Spilman, "Feminist Ideology in the United States: Its Development from 1966-70 as the indicator of a general social movement. Contemporary Crises" June 1978, Volume 2, Issue 2. pp 195-208. https://link.springer.com/article/10.1007/BF02741931
[44] Mari Mikkola, "Feminist Perspectives on Sex and Gender," Stanford Encyclopedia of Philosophy, *Oct 25, 2017.* https://plato.stanford.edu/entries/feminism-gender/#Gender.
[45] "Feminism 101," Red Letter Press, 27 August 2007, http://www.redletterpress.org/feminism101.html.

erased, providing a convenient platform for establishing one of the main objectives of feminism—equalizing the sexes by way of gender roles and functions, in particular. In this way gender as a spectrum becomes justified in the eyes of the philosopher and sociologist. They acknowledge that the differences are clear between males and females from a biological standpoint, yet they relegate gender to human opinion, a completely subjective position, still holding on to the notions of masculinity and femininity. This to me is unjustifiable, super-imposed, gender confusion.

Hereunder is another statement of sheer assumption and supposition:

> However, sociologists and most other social scientists view sex and gender as conceptually distinct. Sex refers to physical or physiological differences between males and females, including both primary sex characteristics (the reproductive system) and secondary characteristics such as height and muscularity. Gender is a term that refers to social or cultural distinctions associated with being male or female.[46]

In the light of the etymology of sex and gender (Chapter 2), where each word, as applied to human beings, means essentially the same, how did the feminists (like the other sociologists) come up with the above distinction? As mentioned in that chapter, the Online Etymology Dictionary shows sex as derived from the Latin sexus meaning the "state of being either male or female," or

---

[46] William Little and Ron McGivern. *Introduction to Sociology*—1st Canadian Edition, p. 366. Rice University, OpenStax College. Creative Commons Attribution 4.0 International License . https://my.uopeople.edu/pluginfile.php/57436/mod_book/chapter/37634/SOC1502.Textbook.pdf.

"the quality of being male or female" (established in 1520).[47] On the other hand, gender (derived from French gendre or genre) means "kind, species; character . . ."; and also 'from the Latin genus meaning race, stock, family; kind, rank, order; species; also '(male or female) sex.'"[48] As was mentioned in chapter 2, this same dictionary makes a salient point, that "gender came to be the usual English word for 'sex of a human being.'"[49] Thus, as applied to human beings, both sex and gender are synonymous.

It should be noted that the word gender was originally used as a grammatical term before it was applied to the male/female dichotomy in the 1500's. According to an online website called The Grammarist,

> Gender was traditionally used mainly in grammar, language, and linguistics contexts to refer to the sex assigned to nouns (especially in non-English languages).[50]

Here is something else of note from the Online Etymology Dictionary concerning the meaning of gender:

> The "male-or-female sex" sense is attested in English from early 15c. As sex (n.) took on erotic qualities in 20c., gender came to be the usual English word for "sex of a human being," in which use it was at first regarded as colloquial or humorous.[51]

In fact, in 1926, Henry Watson Fowler, an English

---
[47] The Online Etymology Dictionary, s.v. *gender*
[48] Ibid.
[49] Ibid.
[50] Gender vs. sex, in the Grammarist. http://grammarist.com/usage/gender-sex/
[51] Online Etymology Dictionary, s.v. gender

lexicographical genius, insisted that gender is grammar-related only. He cautioned, and this author believes that he was dead right:

> Gender...is a grammatical term only. To talk of persons...of the masculine or feminine gender, meaning of the male or female sex, is either a jocularity (permissible or not according to context) or a blunder.[52]

He was indeed prophetic and so accurate, for look at the mess that the world has gotten itself into with the massive gender confusion now engulfing it.

Again, one is constrained to ask the question: Given the etymology of the term gender and the circumstances under which it was introduced to the male/female nomenclature in the 15th to the 20th century, how on earth did sociologists and social scientists come up with, and can be so dogmatic about, such unscientific and purely idealistic notions of gender as opposed to sex? More than that, how could such speculative findings be the basis for societal changes of the magnitude recommended by feminists and other same-sex advocates? Their position seems highly implausible, particularly as the case for gender being different to sex has been shown to be a circular argument as seen in chapter 2.

In yet another article entitled "Feminist Perspectives on Sex and Gender," by Mari Mikkola,[53] the following claim is made:

> Provisionally: 'sex' denotes human females and males depending on biological

---

[52] Henry Watson Fowler in Wikipedia, s.v. gender
[53] Mari Makola, "Feminist Perspectives on Sex and Gender," in Standard Encyclopedia of Psychology. *Oct 25, 2017.* https://plato.stanford.edu/entries/feminism-gender/ 07/02/19.

features (chromosomes, sex organs, hormones and other physical features); 'gender' denotes women and men depending on social factors (social role, position, behaviour or identity).

Again, in the light of the etymology of sex and gender, where each word means essentially the same, and there being no ensuing significant rationale for any alteration, how did Mikkola come up with this distinction?

Hereunder is the real crux of the feminists' agenda as proposed by Gayle Rubin, one of the foremost 2nd wave feminists:

> The dream I find most compelling is one of an androgynous and genderless (though not sexless) society, in which one's sexual anatomy is irrelevant to who one is, what one does, and with whom one makes love [54]

This is the root of all the gender changes proposed by this movement and the many other people that have been influenced by the feminist agenda. It has very little to do with the "discovery of the real meaning" of gender so as to enhance the advancement of human society; it is nothing but a fallacy. It has much more to do with an accommodation for enabling sexual preferences that are unnatural and logically inconceivable.

The truth is that what began as unethical and abominable

---

[54] Scrum_Jet, January 30, 2009, "Gayle Rubin, The Traffic in Women (1975)" (blog), comment on Gayle Rubin, 'The Traffic in Women: Notes on the "Political Economy" of Sex' in Linda Nicholson (ed) *The Second Wave: A Reader in Feminist Theory* (New York and London: Routledge, 1997): 27 – 62. https://purpleprosearchive.wordpress.com/2009/01/30/gayle-rubin-the-traffic-in-women-1975/.

behaviour[55] has now been delusively repackaged via intellectualization and rationalization and presented to contemporary society as "the truth and nothing but the truth." How regrettable! Most people are none the wiser since there is a kind of intellectual idolatry being practiced by the uninformed and naïve around the world. That is, as some people would say: "Whatever the professors say must be right for they are the learned." But is that really so? Look at the sharp lines of demarcation between the 1995 Beijing conference findings and those of the International Criminal Court accord, Rome 1998. Consider the great divide between social scientists and medical or natural scientists. Who are the credible professors here? Which ones are right? Who really are "the learned"?

Yes, the Beijing Conference 1995 focused a lot on human rights, gender fluidity, gender equality and equalizing the sexes, but participants overkilled the subject matter by focusing on equality of roles and functions between men and women rather than equality of value. As we saw before, our Creator established two specific designs of the human anatomy to carry out designated functions in achieving procreation. Once the emphasis is on equalizing roles and functions, one is constrained to seek to remove what same-sex advocates call "stereotypes" for distinguishing males from females. To do so they have to redefine gender as a social construct, artificially shifting its base from sex to a socialization platform.

This is where knowledge of God's Creation mandate and the biblical account as a whole would have solved their dilemma, had their objective been to unearth such knowledge.

---

[55] Levitical code in Holy Bible, Leviticus 18: 22-23: *You shall not lie with a male as with a woman. It is* an abomination. Nor shall you mate with any animal, to defile yourself with it. Nor shall any woman stand before an animal to mate with it. It *is* perversion.

The Creation Account Revisited

For comparison we need to briefly revisit the creation mandate detailed in Chapters 3 and 4 earlier. Recall that in the very act of creation of man, God demonstrated equality of value between the sexes. God's key purpose for creating man was to share His rule or dominion over the earth with man—Gen. 1:26:

> Then God said, "Let Us make man in Our image, according to Our likeness; let them have dominion over the fish of the sea, over the birds of the air, and over the cattle, over all the earth and over every creeping thing that creeps on the earth."

One man could not do this. He therefore established the procreation or sexual reproduction model to ensure that many human beings would be multiplied in the earth for man to exercise that dominion. Thus, He made them male and female.

It should be noted, however, that God made the male man functional first (Gen. 2:7). The woman was "created" at the same time, but in potential form, that is, in the form of a special rib in the ribcage of Adam. Therefore, the woman (Hebr. *nekevah* or y*ishah*) was not an afterthought of God. In God's procreation blueprint, the woman would have played as important a role (although different) as the man, and thus she was to be an integral aspect of the procreation model from the beginning.

God designed the man and placed him in the Garden of Eden to dress and keep it (Gen. 2:8, 15). But one must not lose sight of the fact that the woman was there, tucked away in that ribcage of Adam. Several reasons were pointed out for God making the man functional first. One of these was that God wanted to make a clear statement about who is the leader of the home and society. Secondly, God wanted Adam to discover the unique value of His mate by having him wait longingly and anxiously for her. Adam would have realized that although his role and function as *zakar* was different to hers as *nekevah*, she was invaluable to him to accomplish his purpose. He would have discovered that they were both equal in value, for he could not fulfil the creation mandate without her. Another notable reason was that by initially tucking her away as that special "rib" in the ribcage of Adam (Gen. 2:21-22), God was establishing that a fundamental responsibility of the man was to protect or cover his wife at all times.

Of course, the women of the Beijing Conference 1995 and the feminist movement, because of their lack of knowledge of the Creation account, would have missed the salient point of God creating both men and women equal in value, although different in role and function. The male man has a different functional position to the woman. He is leader of his household; he is the guardian, the guide and the governor of his family; he provides security, love and safety for his household. He is prophet, priest and king of his house.[56]

The man is also designed as the donor of "seed" in the procreation model. The woman, on the other hand, is built to receive the "seed," provide the egg for fertilization and conception, to incubate the young zygote and foetus and develop the baby to the point of delivery. The man and the woman are both unique in their own rights. It is unreasonable, to say the least, even downright absurd or ludicrous, to attempt to equalize their unique functions. Yet that is what the advocates of same-sex unions, backed up by international or multilateral authorities, have been seeking to do. They claim that gender is a social construct, but it is clear rather, that it is a Divine construct and is no different to sex.

Because they failed to see the locus of the real equality issue, the "equal rights" advocates of our world have created a hapless *faux pas*, laying the foundation for a domino effect of evil and rebellious attitudes, behaviours, values, roles and functions. As a result, normal family life is fast becoming an undesirable stereotype in the eyes of an increasing number of people. In

---

[56] Joseph Vernon Duncan, 2002, *The Zakar Man: Male Man in Full Flight*, Zakar Productions TNT Ltd, Arima, Trinidad, p. 48.

the process, society is disintegrating; human dignity is now being reduced to animalistic appetites and lifestyles. Sodomy, lesbianism, and even bestiality are now being celebrated. The unseemly or the inappropriate is now being praised as courage and bravery. It has gone so far that persons have already begun to clamour for the 'right' to be paedophiles. But God has already pronounced a curse on such attitudes:

> Woe to those who call evil good, and good evil; who put darkness for light, and light for darkness; who put bitter for sweet, and sweet for bitter! Woe to those who are wise in their own eyes, and prudent in their own sight! [57]

---

[57] Isa. 5:20-21

7

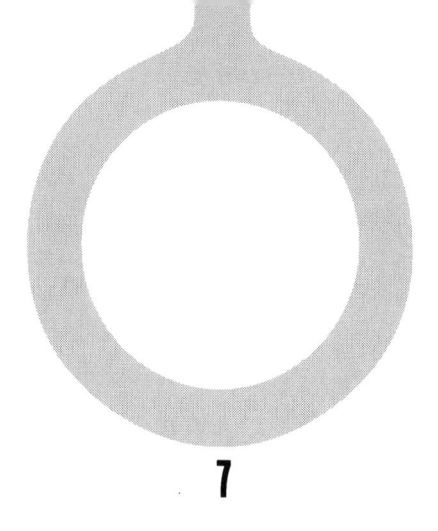

THE SPIRIT OF JEZEBEL:
MALE EMASCULATION IN HISTORICAL PERSPECTIVE

The Jezebel spirit is so called because its death-inflicting venom became fully blown up in perhaps the most notorious woman who ever sat on the throne of Israel or any throne whatsoever—Queen Jezebel. She was the daughter of Ethbaal (literally meaning "with Baal"), King of the Sidonians (1 Kings 16). Israelite king, Ahab, took to wife this woman whose name has become synonymous with "wicked woman" throughout history (Rev. 2:20). She seduced him away from his worship to the true and living God and influenced him to serve and worship her god, Baal; he set up an altar for Baal in the temple of Baal (1 Kings 16:31-32).

So that, instead of aligning herself with Ahab's liturgical practices and acclimatizing to his religious culture, she assumed the position of the religious head of Ahab's household and controlled the worship of the palace. Ethbaal, her father, was most likely a high priest of the Baal cult and Jezebel a priestess; she was also known as a Phoenician princess.[58]

---

[58] Ariela Pelaia, The Story of Jezebel in the Bible: A Worshipper of Baal and Enemy of God," Learn Religions. Updated February 23, 2019. https://www.

According to the biblical account, the worship of Baal also included the worship of the female counterpart, Ashtoreth. In Judges 10:6 we read:

> Then the children of Israel again did evil in the sight of the Lord, and served the Baals and the Ashtoreths, the gods of Syria, the gods of Sidon, the gods of Moab, the gods of the people of Ammon, and the gods of the Philistines; and they forsook the Lord and did not serve Him.

Both Baal and Ashtoreth (sometimes called Asherah) were known as the Phoenicians' fertility god and goddess.[59] Thus sexual ritualism and perversion were rampant in Baal worship during the reign of Jezebel and Ahab. The book of Judges chapter 3 and verse 7 says: "So the children of Israel did evil in the sight of the Lord. They forgot the Lord their God, and served the Baals and Asherahs."

Jezebel had a total of eight hundred and fifty false prophets at her beck and call, according to 1 Kings 18:19:

> [19] Now therefore, send and gather all Israel to me on Mount Carmel, the four hundred and fifty prophets of Baal, and the four hundred prophets of Asherah, who eat at Jezebel's table."[60]

She was a blood-thirsty woman, who was not merely satisfied with taking away the worship of her husband, but was a hater of Israel's God, Yahweh, and sought out and killed thousands of Israel's prophets:

> For so it was, while Jezebel massacred the prophets of the Lord, that Obadiah had taken one hundred prophets and hidden them, fifty to a cave, and had fed them with bread and water (1 Kgs. 18:4).

---

learnreligions.com/who-was-jezebel-2076726. 07/30/19.
[59] "Who was Baal," Got Questions (blog), https://www.gotquestions.org/who-Baal.html. 07/30/19.
[60] Bible, 1 Kings 18:19

Yes, she was a prophet slayer, one who had no hesitation in shedding innocent blood to fulfil her fancy. She was brutal and domineering, unlawfully confiscating property that Ahab himself could only grieve about, but could never legitimately own himself. In 1 Kings chapter 21, she organized to kill Naboth, her own neighbour, to get his vineyard for Ahab, her husband since Naboth would not sell it to Ahab for good reason. The most Ahab could do was to become depressed and sad.

On finding Ahab lying in bed angry, sad and refusing to eat, Jezebel remarked: "You now exercise authority over Israel! Arise, eat food, and let your heart be cheerful; I will give you the vineyard of Naboth the Jezreelite." Jezebel was implying that Ahab did not really know how to use his position as king; her brand of leadership included deadly manipulations. She plotted to get Naboth killed by writing letters to the elders and nobles living in Naboth's city, summoning them to a fast in which Naboth will be given a prominent seat. Two scoundrels would be seated opposite to him who would accuse him of cursing both God and the king. As a result he would be stoned to death.[61]

Jezebel was so powerful that nobody refused to do her bidding. So Naboth was killed. Jezebel then sent word to Ahab that he was now free to possess Naboth's vineyard for he was dead. Such was the heartless and ferocious nature of Jezebel. She was in charge; Ahab was just a figurehead.

In the book of Revelation, Jesus warns His Church about the spirit of Jezebel that would be prominent in these last days:

> **Nevertheless I have a few things against you, because you allow that woman Jezebel, who calls herself a prophetess, to teach and seduce My servants to commit sexual immorality and eat things sacrificed to idols.** [21] **And I gave her time to repent of her sexual immorality, and she did not repent.** [22] **Indeed I will cast her into a sickbed, and those who commit adultery with her into**

---
[61] 1 Kings chapter 21

great tribulation, unless they repent of their deeds. [23] I will kill her children with death, and all the churches shall know that I am He who searches the minds and hearts (Rev. 2:20-23).

The Spirit of Jezebel, Satan's Main Weapon against Manhood

Now, Satan is the arch-rival of the human race. Jesus calls him a murderer from the beginning, a liar, the father of lies (Jn. 8:44), and the thief who has come to steal, to kill and destroy (Jn. 10:10). Satan is fully aware of the legal power of the male man in his rightful position. Thus, once the man is in place as husband, father and head of his household, his authority remains undisputed and cannot be overridden, not even by Satan. Satan needs chaos to function; he cannot manipulate order, let alone Divine order. Jesus Himself endorses the male man as the legal "strongman" of his house when He says: "Or how can one enter a strong man's house and plunder his goods, unless he first binds the strong man? And then he will plunder his house" (Matt. 12:29).

The spirit of Jezebel is a specially assigned demonic principality aimed at belittling, ignoring, overriding, seducing and weakening male leadership in the home and society at large. In effect, that evil spirit reduces the "strongman" to a virtual non-entity, plundering his house. The man's life becomes disordered and so are members of his household; this spills over into society and triggers off mass failure and disaster. Satan's ultimate objective goes beyond destroying male authority to that of utter chaos and the implementation of his deadly manipulative schemes to the family and society at large.

Jezebel in Eden

The truth is that Satan basically dreads the male man as legal head of his house, and therefore, from the beginning of the human race has launched a campaign to remove man from that position of strength. Notice what played out in the Garden of Eden when Satan in the form of the serpent beguiled our first parents. Here is the account (Gen. 3:1-6):

> Now the serpent was more cunning than any beast of the field which the Lord God had made. And he said to the woman, "Has God indeed said, 'You shall not eat of every tree of the garden'?" ² And the woman said to the serpent, "We may eat the fruit of the trees of the garden; ³ but of the fruit of the tree which is in the midst of the garden, God has said, 'You shall not eat it, nor shall you touch it, lest you die.' "⁴ Then the serpent said to the woman, "You will not surely die. ⁵ For God knows that in the day you eat of it your eyes will be opened, and you will be like God, knowing good and evil." ⁶ So when the woman saw that the tree was good for food, that it was pleasant to the eyes, and a tree desirable to make one wise, she took of its fruit and ate. She also gave to her husband with her, and he ate.

Now pay attention to the fact that Eve was comprehensively deceived right before the very eyes of her husband. Why did Adam not defend her and save the human race from plunging into sin? There may be several reasons. First, Adam was not a natural conversationalist (not used to speaking much) as Eve was (attested to in the meaning of "help meet" in chapter 4); second, Adam might have felt himself inadequate to deal with the subtlety of Satan. Third, he could have been in a state of shock owing to Satan's intentional disregard for him as head of the woman, bypassing him and addressing her directly.

In the opinion of this writer, Satan, in this bizarre act, was primarily waging psychological warfare against the man, although this did not seem to be as blatant as his seduction of the woman. He knew fully well that God had spoken directly to the man about not eating of the tree of knowledge of good and evil. Thus, if he approached Adam with the question, "Did God say?" the man would have bluntly answered "Yes, God said." Therefore, he confronted Eve. She did not hear directly from God so she was more vulnerable to his subtlety. He quickly capitalized on her inevitable ambivalence, and gave his own verdict concerning the consequences of eating from the tree. The woman fell for it, and was hoodwinked through the lust of the flesh (the tree was "good for food"), the lust of the eyes (the tree was "pleasant to the eyes"), and the pride of life ("desirable to make one wise"). She ate of the tree and "gave to her husband with her and he ate".[62]

Indeed, while one would be inclined to focus more on Satan's deception of Eve, one must not overlook the psychological warfare against Adam. The implied message to Adam could have been: "You are not essential here; you are low-ranking and inconsequential; she is the key person, let me ask her instead." That silent message would have most likely demoralized Adam and caused him to think less of himself at that moment. His leadership role was undermined. The male man was relegated to a secondary role in a crucial decision-making exercise through the commandeering of authority by the woman under the influence of Lucifer. Whenever authority is misappropriated and falls into the wrong hands, disaster is inevitable. Thus, that Jezebel spirit (epitomized in Queen Jezebel) assigned by Satan to emasculate or reduce the male man to that of a mere figurehead was birthed right there in Eden.

Jezebel in Post-modern Philosophy

That same disarmament principle of the male man is rampant in post-modern human society today, where the male man is stripped from his leadership role and morphed into an unimaginable weak and feeble version of manhood. This is the diabolical modus operandi of the kingdom of darkness, fully characteristic of the Jezebel spirit; Jezebel was the woman in whom that male-destroying spirit reached its zenith. In today's world, this hell-bent principality is given more than enough room to work its devastating spell on the head of the family, the

---
[62] Cf. 1 Jn. 2:15-17

family itself, the Church and society as a whole; most people are oblivious of its existence. The quicker mankind could awake and identify this deceptive and deadly spirit, the better we would be able to make sense of the quagmire that society is in right now. Otherwise, Satan would continue to shift authority from the male man. He would continue to feminize human society as he emasculates the man. In this way, he could have an easier legal passage to manipulate and destroy the human race.

Jezebel in the Slave Trade

It is well documented in various online sources and history books that male African slaves were generally used as "studs." Stud-breeding was a integral part of the slave trade, where a strong, healthy black man would be placed in a room full of black women to impregnate them with slave children for his master. His masa valued him highly, that is, as one of his prized possessions, because of his sexual prowess. There are accounts of male slaves being hired for this purpose. In several quarters, men and boys were deprived of wearing pants, and viewed more in the vein of sex machines. In other words, the emasculation of the male man was extremely intense in the slave trade. Indeed, the spirit of Jezebel was rampant in this God-forbidden practice of stripping the male man from his dignity and integrity.

That mentality has persisted in the black family even today. There has been a perpetuation of that stud mentality where it is common for a lot of our black brothers (married or not) to be sexually active with numerous women at the same time. This is viewed as machoism by most men who are practicing this free-for-all sexual lifestyle, but at the end it enslaves them. The curse has been handed down, unabated from generation to generation. The fathers have influenced the sons, and although masa is no longer around, the originally forced practice has now become engrained and habitual. More than that, many men have become brutal to their women, belittling them in value, another slave trade fallout. The low value of women was especially evident in the slave trade. Thus, with regard to the contemporary black man, the level of emasculation is alarming, gravely affecting himself, his family and society at large. God is the greatest hope for the black man, and the male man in general. He is the only one who could restore his dignity and fill the missing links in his life.

Jezebel in the Struggle for Women's Rights

In light of the foregoing, one must be reminded that the official platform for the redefinition of gender as a social construct, and the subsequent recommendations to governments around the world, was the "Fourth World Conference on Women Beijing 1995." It is that redefinition that has basically catapulted worldwide lifestyle changes and given full sanction to the LBTQI... community in many quarters. Doubtlessly, the input of men in this major social issue was minimal. It is mind-bugging how a crucial issue like this, with such far reaching consequences for male/female identity and behaviour, could be made largely without male input. That the decision was then consciously or subconsciously endorsed by the men of our society with little or no resistance is incomprehensible.

Like in the Garden of Eden, men have simply stood by and agreed with the baseless manoeuvring of the women of the United Nations to make gender into a social construct. The women called the shots for such a radical and widespread change in society, making a decision to alter society as a whole, while men said nothing. What a travesty of authority!

I do not want to come across as a male chauvinist but it is clear that Satan has again succeeded in misapplying the authority of women to disrupt God's moral and ethical order. Because Satan has desensitized men concerning their legal position in the home and society, the male man is generally not alert to the manoeuvrings going on around him. He has been duped and does not even know it. He is easily manipulated into surrendering his masculinity, his rights to leadership and decision-making, his unique role as husband, father and protector of his household. Many men have surrendered their position as prophet, priest and king of their homes, plunging the natural family and the human race as a whole into utter chaos as we now see. The male-derogating spirit of Jezebel is at work; those who have eyes to see must see before it is too late.

Jezebel Bore an Uncanny Resemblance to Semiramis, Her Distant Ancestor

In the book of I Kings chapter 16, cited earlier, Jezebel is identified as the daughter of Ethbaal, king of the Sidonians; that is, she was a distant descendent of Sidon, son of Canaan and son of Ham, one of three sons of Noah. Genesis chapter 9 tells us that Ham was the son who committed a hideous act against his father when he found him drunk and naked in his tent from an overdose of wine. Exactly what Ham did is a matter of conjecture since the Bible does not explain it. Nevertheless, the Scripture says in verses 24-25:

> So Noah awoke from his wine, and knew what his younger son had done to him. [25] Then he said: "Cursed be Canaan; a servant of servants he shall be to his brethren."

It should be noted that Canaan was not yet born when Noah pronounced the curse on him. It should also be reasonable to believe that although there was no direct words said to Ham in the form of a curse, his very act against his father would have relegated him and his bloodline to a curse. History has shown that the Hamitic line has been known for much evil and some of the most hideous abominations. The cities of Sodom and Gomorrah, notorious for homosexuality and wanton promiscuity (Gen. 19), which God destroyed with fire and brimstone, were part of Hamitic territory (Gen. 10:15-19).

Ham had another son called Cush. He was the father of Nimrod, who built the tower of Babel, according to Genesis chapter 10 verse 8 to 11 and Genesis chapter 11. The name Nimrod means "rebel," for he opposed "God's righteous governing authority."[63] Nimrod's wife (his own mother) was Semiramis, one of the most corrupt and degenerate women who ever lived.[64] Thus the curse of incest and a myriad of sexual abominations characterized the rebellion of Nimrod and his wife. Although her name is not mentioned in Scripture, she is well-known in ancient history according to various online sources. She is still revered by many even today. Much of what she was known for—queen of heaven, mother of god, etc.—has been virtually incarnated in a succession of female deities of religious cults throughout the ages, including Jezebel.

From the standpoint of her worldview, Semiramis was anti-God, totally rebellious and downright satanic.[65] According to legend, she was in charge of the religious rituals of the palace and had a network of evil priests under her influence (similar to Jezebel). Being a former harlot, she became pregnant while married to Nimrod. When she found out that he wanted to dethrone her and expose the truth, she carefully devised a murderous plot to sacrifice him instead of the fatted ram offered every year. She instructed her loyal priests to grab Nimrod at the call for the sacrifice. They dismembered him as they would have done the ram.

According to the writings of Noah Hutchings,

all of the body was cut up and scattered with the exception of his reproductive organs. It was from this ancient and obscure Babylonian tradition that the worship of the "phallus" began.[66]

---

[63] "Discover the Biblical Character of Nimrod," Step into the Glory from Genesis to Revelation. https://stepintothestory.ca/know-nimrod-married-mother/
[64] Ibid.
[65] Ibid.
[66] Noah W. Hutchings, The Persian Gulf Crisis and the Final Fall of Babylon. Hearthstone Publishing, Oklahoma, 1990, p. 53.

Hutchings cites The Encyclopedia of Religions (Vol. 3, p. 264) to reveal: "Queen Semiramis in Babylon erected an obelisk one hundred thirty feet high to the memory of Nimrod."[67] This is confirmed in an online blog which says: "Queen Semiramis erected a 130-foot obelisk in Babylon and it was associated with sun worship and represented the phallus of the sun god Baal or Nimrod."[68] In other words, in the mind of Semiramis, Nimrod was only good for his phallus, nothing more; nothing else in him was deserving of celebration. Many post-modern women think the same thing of men.

Notwithstanding, most men do not help the situation by their wayfaring sexual escapades, resulting in nothing but vanity as the wise man puts it in the book of Ecclesiastes. As we suggested earlier in this book, without a well-developed worship component the man is reduced to a sex monger. He is often overwhelmed and virtually helpless when his sexual drive and phallic passion are aroused. He is a sitting duck for exploitation and seduction without a sound relationship with his God. We were designed to work in harmony with our Creator, having been made in His own image and likeness (Gen. 1:26); without Him we are easily lead astray.

The Obelisk: Worship of the Male Phallus

The word obelisk is defined as "an upright 4-sided usually monolithic pillar that gradually tapers as it rises and terminates in a pyramid."[69] It is said also to mean "Baal's shaft" or "Baal's organ of reproduction."[70] In plain language, the obelisk is an image that represents an erect phallus; thus it is a sex symbol. It is used around the world to remember certain prominent men,

---

[67] Ibid.
[68] "Seed of Nimrod and Semiramis," 18th October, 2012. https://goccuk321.blogspot.com/2012/10/seed-of-nimrod-semiramis.html.
[69] Merriam Webster, s.v. *obelisk*
[70] Michael Scheiffer, "Pagan Sun Worship and Catholicism: The Pagan Sun Wheel, the Obelisk and Bal," citing *Masonic and Occult Symbols Illustrated by Dr. Cathy Burns*, p. 341). http://www.aloha.net/~mikesch/wheel.htm. 07/30/19.

and by many ritualistic cults to represent Baal. Whatever else it represents, it is certain that it suggests that the male sexual organ is "a god" and that it should be worshipped. That is one of the ways that Satan steals his own worship—through sexual seduction, deception and exploitation of the male man.

Obelisks and Male Nudity Around the World

Surprise! Surprise! the Washington Monument on Capitol Hill is an obelisk. There is an obelisk in Central Park, New York; there are several in the city of Rome. A large number of them decorate the skyline of Egypt, and several other locations throughout the world. So picture a typical visit to the Washington Monument. In reality, the "ooh's"" and "wows" emitting from the admirers of such a magnificent work of architecture are the open adorations of the erect penis. Totally oblivious to the average person, such unwitting worship of the male phallus no doubt stimulates the realm of sexually perversed spirits. In the process, sexual promiscuity and exploitation of all forms are promoted. Think about the distorting impact on human dignity and morality, the sacrilegious, unrestricted and uncensored showcasing of male sexuality that such adoration generates. This has the effect of reducing the male man's significance to nothing but sexual.

There should be no guessing then why our world is so sex-crazy. It seems logical to conclude that the greater the sacrilegious homage given to the male phallus, the greater would be the sexual pollution and the playboy mentality pervading society. The male man would be increasingly out of control sexually, leaving in his trail many vanquished subjects, including himself. Women, on the other hand, would be reactionary, gravitating to all forms of unwholesome practices and outright abominations themselves. Protest movements like feminism would certainly mushroom under these circumstances. What a grave tragedy for the human race, mainly because of its flirtation with the kingdom of darkness!

Thus the atmospheres over our cities are saturated with

sexual demonic forces by virtue of the obelisks piercing the skylines. Many church steeples, unknowing to parishioners, represent a form of the obelisk, so that almost automatically the sacred and the profane are mixed. What a twisted and contorted world in which to live! Indeed, deception is one of Satan's master weapons.

For different reasons, there are references to obelisks in the Bible: They are called "sacred pillars." Pay attention to the following verses: Deuteronomy 16:2: "You shall not set up a sacred pillar, which the Lord your God hates;" Hosea 10:2: "Their heart is divided; now they are held guilty. He will break down their altars; He will ruin their sacred pillars;" Micah 5:13: "I will cut off your carved images and your sacred pillars from among you, so that you will no longer bow down to the work of your hands;" 1Kings 14:23 (AMP): "For they also built for themselves high places [to worship idols] and sacred pillars and Asherim [for the goddess Asherah]."

Indeed, the sexual perversion, characteristic of Semiramis has come down through the ages from generation to generation, infiltrating societies and communities across the globe. That spirit became more popularized in Jezebel, but it is basically the same spirit that Satan employed way back in the Garden of Eden to emasculate the male man. The book review by Derek Beres of Guy Garcia's book, "The Decline of Men: How the American Male Is Tuning Out, Giving Up, and Flipping Off His Future," should provide for some interesting reading."[71] Beres refers to Garcia's concern with "a cultural deflation in the masculinity of our times."[72]

---

[71] Derek Beres, "The Decline of Men: How the American Male Is Tuning Out, Giving Up, and Flipping Off His Future,"18 March, 2009. Popmatters. https://www.popmatters.com/66805-the-decline-of-men-how-the-american-male-is-tuning-out-giving-up-and--2496094535.html.
[72] Ibid.

Raw Evidence from this Writer's Recent European Tour

During a recent European tour, this writer had the opportunity of visiting three historical sites that confirmed the truism of historical male emasculation—the Eiffel Tower in Paris, the Vatican city in Rome and the ruins of the ancient city of Pompeii in Naples, Italy.

The Eiffel Tower. Unknowing to many, the Eiffel tower is a massive obelisk, yet one of the biggest tourist attractions in Paris. Throngs of people visit that site on a daily basis and are astounded by the magnificence of this prodigious work of art, oblivious of the adulation being paid to the male phallus.

The Vatican city. An obelisk 132 feet high, said to be a gift from Egypt, stands in the centre of the St. Peter's Square, with a cross atop. It was brought to Rome by Emperor Caligula in AD 37.[73] It was at first placed in the circus, south of the basilica, but finally relocated to the middle of St. Peter's square in 1586 by order of Pope Sixtus V.[74] This obelisk stands only two feet higher than that of Semiramis', and is positioned in the centre of a circle at its base, representing "the female vagina and thus male/female duality."[75] In this writer's opinion, there seems to be an unmistakable blend of the sacred and the profane here.

A tour through the Vatican museum revealed many extravagant displays of marble motifs of male nudity, virtually everywhere, all under the rubric of art. There were at least two motifs, said to be depicting Greek mythology, that showed images of men as well as those of half man and half beast (centaurs) engaged in a wild sexual scene.

Another display was one depicting a sexual struggle among

---

[73] "The Obelisk," St Peters Basilica Info. http://www.stpetersbasilica.info/Exterior/Obelisk/Obelisk.htm
[74] Ibid.
[75] "Locations of Obelisks Around the world," Free Thinkers. https://www.tapatalk.com/groups/free_thinkers/locations-of-obelisks-around-the-world-t6278.html

nude males and females, one of the men all but grabbing the genitals of another male, while he struggles to get at one of the women. By the way, the legs of the biggest and most muscular male image in the pact were snake-like—a hint of reductionism of the male man to an animalistic imagery? Greek mythology or not, what are the impressions left by these displays on the psyche of both male and female adults, not to mention vulnerable youth—just curious artforms? I seriously doubt. Surprisingly, and for whatever reasons, one did not see as a rule displays of female nudity at this museum.

It does not take high science to explain why the men of the cloth are having such a morbid struggle with their sexuality. It is difficult to imagine them not falling into the snare of sexual perversion under the circumstances. That is why Jesus commissioned His Church to be the light of the world (Matt. 5:16) and not a participant of the unfruitful works of darkness (Eph. 5:11): "And have no fellowship with the unfruitful works of darkness, but rather expose them."

The Ancient City of Pompeii. Our visit to Pompeii further exacerbated the notion that one of Satan's major objectives is to emasculate the male man and make him into a playboy rather than allow him to be the legal strongman and leader of his home and society. We learned that Pompeii was an ancient hillside city; it was first destroyed by a massive earthquake around 62 A.D. The survivors of this earthquake focused their energy on rebuilding the city. They were well on their way to restoring its farms, vineyards, industrial and commercial centres when on a day in August 79 A.D. disaster again struck. This time it was total annihilation, via the violent eruption of a nearby volcano, sealing the demise of Pompeii. Amazingly, this volcano was inactive for centuries and believed to be completely dead, but it suddenly erupted, raining down on Pompeii and neighbouring towns lava and volcanic ash to a depth of about 25 feet in some places. For almost 2000 years this city had remained buried, even though surrounding cities, like Naples, were rebuilt. Consensus is that there has been a fear associated with restoring it, perhaps because of the close proximity and the nature of the two devastating disasters that occurred.

During our tour of the ruins of Pompeii, it became clear to us why this ancient city was destroyed. Excavation of the buried city did not begin until about 1600 years after the killer volcano struck, which no occupant of the city survived. Through our tour guide, we learned that by the work of skilled archaeologists, like Guiseppe Fiorelli, most of the ruins had been uncovered. There was evidence in the city itself that, as it was in the case of Sodom and Gomorrah, God Himself rained fire, hot larva and volcanic ash on the city in judgment for the depth of sexual abominations into which the people had sunken. Pieces of melted sulphur could be seen everywhere. We learned that prostitution was a huge business enterprise in the city. To confirm this, we saw remains of the lupanare (house of the prostitute), comprising of five rooms, each outfitted with a stone bed and pillow (intact).

After passing through the lupanare, and walking through the streets leading up to it, we had the shock of our lives. Our guide asked us if we wanted to see the beginning of GPS technology, pointing to a carving of a male phallus on a side wall on the street, showing the way to the lupanare. On another cross street, there was also a carving of a male phallus, this time on a stone lying flat on the street, again pointing in the direction of the whorehouse. In exiting the city, we could only conclude: "Man is certainly blind and hard of hearing," for positioned right at the highest point at the western end of the ruined city is a stature of a stark naked male, about 40 feet in height, overlooking the adjoining city of Naples. This was a gift by a famous sculptor not very long ago. The statue simply, and in plain language, depicts the sexual perversion for which that ancient city was known, and explains why God had to destroy it. In fact, in the tourist market place, just as one enters the ruined city, moulded images of the erect male phallus were on sale as "good luck" artefacts. That is the imagery to which Satan has always wanted to reduce the man—total emasculation, devoid of dignity, honour and respect, good for nothing but his sexual power. Father God, save this generation.

The historical perspective of male emasculation by way of seduction and its awful consequences is clear from the foregoing accounts. If this generation fails to learn from the past, then we are doomed to repeat it (re George Satanaya —1905).

Hope is Still Alive, However

There is hope for God-ordained family life in these last days as implied in the book of Malachi chapter 4, verses 5-6:

> Behold, I will send you Elijah the prophet before the coming of the great and dreadful day of the Lord. [6] And he will turn the hearts of the fathers to the children, and the hearts of the children to their fathers, lest I come and strike the earth with a curse.

God's message to us in these verses is that just before the coming of Jesus, He will send the spirit of Elijah to His Church to restore normal family life in the earth—"turn the hearts of the fathers to the children and the hearts of the children to their fathers." Elijah was the prophet in history who stood up for righteousness and challenged the status quo ruled by Queen Jezebel. He brought her and Ahab to an open shame on Mt. Carmel, when he proved that the living God Yahweh could answer by fire after Baal failed to show up.

Here is the deal that Elijah made, as recorded in 1 Kings chapter 18:

> [23] Therefore let them give us two bulls; and let them choose one bull for themselves, cut it in pieces, and lay it on the wood, but put no fire under it; and I will prepare the other bull, and lay it on the wood, but put no fire under it. [24] Then you call on the name of your gods, and I will call on the name of the Lord; and the God who answers by fire, He is God."

They agreed to the challenge because they believed they could do it. Elijah gave them first preference. Nothing happened. In frustration, they began to cut themselves:

> [28] So they cried aloud, and cut themselves, as was their custom, with knives and lances, until the blood gushed out on them. [29] And when midday was past, they prophesied until the time of the offering of the evening sacrifice. But there was no voice; no one answered, no one paid attention.

Then, it was Elijah's turn:

> [32] Then with the stones he built an altar in the name of the Lord; and he made a trench around the altar large enough to hold two seahs of seed. [33] And he put the wood in order, cut the bull in pieces, and laid it on the wood, and said, "Fill four waterpots with water, and pour it on the burnt sacrifice and on the wood." [34] Then he said, "Do it a second time," and they did it a second time; and he said, "Do it a third time," and they did it a third time. [35] So the water ran all around the altar; and he also filled the trench with water.

Then Elijah prayed to Yahweh:

> Lord God of Abraham, Isaac, and Israel, let it be known this day that You are God in Israel and I am Your servant, and that I have done all these things at Your word. [37] Hear me, O Lord, hear me, that this people may know that You are the Lord God, and that You have turned their hearts back to You again. [38] Then the fire of the Lord fell and consumed the burnt sacrifice, and the wood and the stones and the dust, and it licked up the water that was in the trench. [39] Now when all the people saw it, they fell on their faces and they said: "The Lord, He is God! The Lord, He is God!"

Now that is the anointing and enablement that God has

promised for His people in these last days. It is confrontational, defiant and demonstrative of God's superior authority working through His Church. The spirit of Elijah has the unenviable task of confronting and defeating the Jezebel spirit and exposing the Baal myth. In the light of the foregoing, I believe that God will dismantle the man-made, artificial versions of the family now being made popular. God's plans shall not be thwarted. God has promised through His prophet Malachi that there would be a Divine revolution and a return to normal family life as He planned it from the beginning.

8

WHO IS STEALING OUR FATHERS?

At the end of the last chapter we saw hints of a paternal crisis in these last days, strongly implied through the words of the prophet Malachi. In this chapter, I wish to expound some more on this scriptural passage.

> Behold, I will send you Elijah the prophet before the coming of the great and dreadful day of the Lord. [6] And he will turn the hearts of the fathers to the children, and the hearts of the children to their fathers, lest I come and strike the earth with a curse.

The fact that God mentions the restoration of the hearts of the fathers with the hearts of the children helps us to understand the crisis of the fathers in the last days. In my book, The Zakar Man: Male Man in Full Flight,[76] I pointed out that Satan employs a strategy similar to normal warfare, that of getting the king first. Once the enemy gets the king, the will is blown out of the opposing army, so to speak. If you kill the captain, the war is over.

In the light of the above, Satan may also use an indirect

---

[76] Joseph Vernon Duncan, 2002, The Zakar Man: Male Man in Full Flight, pp. 58-63 (Arima: Trinidad).

approach to keeping the man away from his stronghold.[77] Your stronghold could be seen, in a sense, as the thing you were born to do, the place from which you can fight best. Since the male man by definition is competent to worship, then true worship constitutes his stronghold. His primary place of worship is his home. I also mentioned in *Zakar Man: Male Man in Full Flight* that ". . . if you can function in the thing that you were born for and designed for, that is where you are going to be strongest."[78]

Just take a look around and see the phenomenon right before your eyes. There are male fallouts everywhere. Men can hardly be found at home, the primary place of worship. In many cases, even if men are present in person at home, they are not concerned. In several other cases, they are brutal to mother and children. In addition, men are a rarity in the school system where young lives who missed fathering at home could be further nurtured; there is a universal dearth of male teachers in our schools. A similar situation exists in the Church; men are hardly at church, the place where they could develop their worship competence. There has to be a mastermind behind this.

In short, men could hardly be found where a positive impact on the development of young vulnerable lives is needed. In general, men shy away from anything resembling spirituality, nurturing and reinforcing core values of life to the young ones; or, from any place linked to these things. Based on the myth that "big men don't cry," men do not want to associate with things that appear to be emotional; yet ironically, men are the most vociferous and enthusiastic in the field of sports. There is a real deception here.

What is, or rather who is, responsible for this awful fate of the male man? The truth is that there is a thief on the prowl, who is bent on destroying the human race by any means possible. Jesus, referring to Satan, says it thus: "The thief does not come except to steal, and to kill, and to destroy. I have come that they

---
[77] Ibid.
[78] Ibid.

may have life, and that they may have it more abundantly"(Jn. 10:10). Earlier in the book of John, Jesus warned us about Satan::

> He was a murderer from the beginning, and does not stand in the truth, because there is no truth in him. When he speaks a lie, he speaks from his own resources, for he is a liar and the father of I (Jn. 8:44).

The prophet Malachi tells us that a curse would be in the earth if the hearts of the fathers are torn from the children and vice versa. That is exactly what we are seeing now. What is a curse? A curse is a rhythm of failure, that is, whatever one attempts to do culminates with failure and disaster. This scenario surrounds us in our society today. The prophet Malachi is informing us that the real reason for such a debacle in human society is the virtual ripping apart of the hearts of the fathers from the children and vice versa. With the onslaught of the LBGTIQ ideology and the increasing rebellion against God's creative order, the foregoing is exactly what has happened. The Genesis model of the natural or normal family is ignored as traditional and archaic. Notwithstanding, the prophet Malachi seems to imply that in these last days there is hope for the normal or natural family as God Himself instituted it in Genesis 2:24: "Therefore shall a man leave his father and his mother, and shall cleave unto his wife: and they shall be one flesh" (KJV).

The Impact of Male Fallout in the Home

The home is regarded as the basic unit of society. Society is as good as its homes. Since Satan as the thief has come to steal, to kill and destroy, then one would expect him to start with the family. However, in order to destroy the family, he has to destroy the legal head, the male man (the father), the "strongman" as we saw earlier. The male of the family is target *numero uno* for Satan. As we hinted earlier, if Satan could remove, immobilize, dislodge or disorient the "strongman," it becomes very easy to destroy the rest of the family, since their security, their guard and covering is rendered ineffective. In some cases, the father may be completely unknown. This means no prophet, no priest, and no king of the household to ensure the family's well-being.

The ultimate consequences of the foregoing are the absence of love, care, safety and sound values such as compassion, sharing, morality, ethics or spiritual values. These deficiencies result in a range of generational curses, accompanied by fear, anxiety, tension, anger, bitterness and low self-esteem, among other alarming features. For a more detailed understanding of generational curses and how to uproot them, see my book: "The Five Laws of Generational Curses: Uprooting Them."[79]

Impact on the Young Male

More specifically, for the young male, there is no real hero to emulate as a result of the lack of fathering. A male crisis in the home means a leadership crisis in society, since men are the divinely designated head of the home and not merely a societal choice, as some schools of thought have it. In the face of poor fathering, young men become resentful, rebellious, powerless, and lack confidence. In the young man's mad hunt for power (a natural quest of all men), the gang leader becomes the surrogate father, who empowers him. The father is the one who holds the responsibility of empowering his son. The gang becomes the substitute family, and crime becomes his "domestic duties," so to speak. The gun and the knife then become symbols of the power that could not be obtained from the young man's father or guardian.

In addition, serious distortions of love and passion translate into rape, incest and all forms of sexual molestation, as the young male seeks to attest his masculinity or male prowess. He is disoriented and, therefore, does not know how to love or receive love. He finds it extremely difficult or awkward to give true love to his wife or receive love from her, if he never saw his father extend loving care to his mother. He becomes indiscrete

---

[79] Available at Amazon.com

and undisciplined, driven by his phallus rather than true love, becoming a phallic man rather than a loving and committed one. Masturbation, pornography, cybersex, homosexuality and abnormal sexual passions become a way of life for him. His phallus in many cases becomes an object of uncontrolled self-gratification, and a weapon of destruction rather than a sacred instrument of true love.

The foregoing disorientation makes the young man vulnerable to abominations of all kinds. His sexual emotions became confused and erratic, in some cases dangerously impulsive. These are the real roots of sexual perversion and so-called sexual orientation, homosexuality, bestiality and other abnormal and unwholesome sexual appetites. All these phenomena should be more properly labelled as sexual disorientation rather than sexual orientation. Same-sex advocates have it all wrong; they have flipflopped truth and reality for their own version of human relations.

Impact on the Young Female

In terms of young women, the deprivation of fatherhood, whether through absenteeism (physically present, absent or being totally unknown), brutality, or other forms of abuse, affect them in innumerable ways. Within recent times, incest has become a real menace, in which blood fathers or stepfathers, even elder or younger brothers sexually abuse young girls, teenagers and young adults. The damage done is often immeasurable and create life-long wounds.

Many young women, as a psychological kick-back, go on an elusive and risky search for the father they never had. In the process, their emotions and psyches are severely ravaged by the exploitation of the "sugar-daddies" and pimps of our day. Such young women tend to develop a dependency syndrome. They become attracted to the older men because they are capable of providing them with more financial perks and other mostly temporary comforts. Regrettably, however, these young ladies are prone to contracting HIV/AIDs and other STDs from these older men, who have been around and are greater carriers of these health menaces. Recent statistics in Trinidad and Tobago show: "In the age group 15-19 years, six times as many young women as young men have HIV,"[80] proof that they are sleeping more with older men than with their teenage counterparts.

Moreover, it is within this debacle of absentee fatherhood that the seeds of prostitution, lesbianism and bestiality find rich soil in which to germinate and develop. Many of these social ills stem from poor values. In prostitution, young women are searching for personal security; in lesbianism, they are on a false quest for true love; bestiality demonstrates the debt of abomination that one would indulge in to fill the empty void left by psychological damage. The phenomenon of runaway girls is often linked to the double effect of sexual abuse and not being believed, not even by mother.

Male Fallout in Education

According to several online sources, over the past quarter-century, the number of female undergrads in the United States has grown twice as fast as males. The Hechinger report of 2017 indicates that in that fall, women would have comprised more than 56% of all students in colleges in the United States, according to the U.S. Department of Education.[81] This represents 2.2 million less men than women enrolled in that year. That same report reveals that 50% of the business degrees were to be awarded to women[82]. Is there something happening here that we all need to know?

---

[80] Early Sexual Activity Raises HIV Risks for Trinidad and Tobago Girls https://www.prb.org/earlysexualactivityraiseshivriskfortrinidadandtobagogirls/.
[81] Jon Marcus, "Why Men Are the New College Minority," *The Atlantic,* Aug. 8, 2017
[82] Ibid.

Male Fallout to Penal Institutions

Moreover, there is a significant loss of men from normal productive life to the prison system as a result of crime. Recent statistics indicate that in the United States, the Federal prison population consists of 93.2% men to 6.8% women,[83] giving further credence to this author's argument that there is a thief around, and he is stealing our fathers. Recent figures in Trinidad and Tobago show a prison population of 3999, of which 97.1% (approximately 3883) are men.[84] Who is stealing our fathers? Can somebody answer?

Poor Personality Development

Fatherlessness could have a detrimental effect on personality development. There are various theories on personality development. One school of thought is that by six years of age, 85% of a child's personality is already formed; by ten years of age, 100 % of a person's personality is formed. Another recent statistic indicates that a child's personality is set for life by the time he or she is in first grade (6-7 years of age).[85] That is, by this tender juncture in life, the basic tenets of one's personality are already established from a unique combination of genetic (temperament) and environmental factors. Personality is formed around values. The father is generally regarded as the reinforcer of such values in the home. Thus, personality development could be increasingly warped depending on the degree of fatherlessness of the child.

---

[83] Dyfed Loesche, "The Prison Gender Gap," Oct 23, 2017, Statista https://www.statista.com/chart/11573/gender-of-inmates-in-us-federal-prisons-and-general-population/
[84] World Prison Brief Data for Trinidad and Tobago, 18 Sept, 2018, World Prison Brief, Institute of Criminal Policy Research, Birkbeck University, London. https://www.prisonstudies.org/country/trinidad-and-tobago.
[85] Life Science Staff, "Personality Set for Life by First Grade," Life Science, August 6, 2010. https://www.livescience.com/8432-personality-set-life-1st-grade-study-suggests.html

Maleness Signifies Sacredness

We pointed out before that the Hebrew word *zakar* used for male man in Genesis 1:27 carries a dual significance—sharp male organ and competence to worship (chapter 3).[86] Thus maleness, in its core value, is linked to sacredness and holiness. Proof of this is in Genesis 17:10-11, where God required Abraham to cut off the foreskin of his phallus to mark covenant with Him:

> [10] This is My covenant which you shall keep, between Me and you and your descendants after you: Every male child among you shall be circumcised; [11] and you shall be circumcised in the flesh of your foreskins, and it shall be a sign of the covenant between Me and you.

Of all the parts of the human body, God could find no other suitable symbol but the foreskin of the penis for this sacred covenant. In the eyes of God, therefore, the male genital has deep spiritual implications. Therefore a man ought not to use his phallus merely for self-aggrandizement or emotional satisfaction and ignore its sacredness. It is sacred chiefly because of its God-ordained function to produce seed for the perpetuation of the human species created after God's own image and likeness. The significance of the male genital (equally so the female womb) goes beyond mere pleasure.

Maleness Means Spiritual Leadership

By virtue of Adam being made functional first, one would expect that the first voice to be heard worshipping God in the Garden of Eden was that of the man. In addition, since by definition he is competent to worship, the man is the spiritual leader of his household, that is, the prophet priest and king of his house.[87] It should be noted that the word *zakar* is not a Christian

---

[86] Francis Brown, S.R. Driver, Charles A. Briggs, Hebrew and English Lexicon of the Old Testament, s.v. zakar and nekevah.

[87] More is said of this in my book, Zakar Man: Male Man in Full Flight.

terminology; it is Hebrew language and not a religious vernacular. It is who the male man is regardless of his religion. All male men are defined by their sexuality and their worship. This is the basic identity of the man and should eliminate the enigma and the mystery surrounding the male man.

Man's Sexuality and Worship Must Be Balanced

With man's fall, he lost spiritual connection with God and therefore was deprived of his privilege to worship God. As a result, he became depraved in his very nature. Nevertheless, his propensity for worship propelled him to worship any way. Virtually everything became the object of fallen man's worship, even his own sexuality, allowing for the mushrooming of grave transgressions, including sexual perversions and abominations in human society.

While the practice of man's true worship to God was curtailed because of sin, severely reducing his ability to communicate with God, and rendering him spiritually inept, his physical attributes, including his sexuality, remained intact. The problem with this is that the man became woefully imbalanced with only half of his definition realized. The truth is that without worship the male man is only half of his true identity.. Consequently, there is very little left to temper his sexuality. The latter, therefore, could easily get out of control, mainly because of the extremely strong driving force of male sexuality. True worship was provided by our wise Creator to put male sexuality in its rightful context.

Thus, like a motor car running on two left side or right side wheels down the highway, the male man cannot sustain himself merely by his sexuality, in spite of how strong he thinks he is. He soon careens into a ditch and crashes. Worship brings the man back on the road, so to speak, and adds dignity and sacred balance to his sexuality. This is where Satan has specifically targeted the male man—to prevent him from worshipping. Notwithstanding, God has made a way for man to be reconciled to Him, as the following scriptural passages reveal:

John 3:16: For God so loved the world that He gave His only begotten Son, that whoever believes in Him should not perish but have everlasting life.

1 Peter 1:18-20: knowing that you were not redeemed with corruptible things, like silver or gold, from your aimless conduct received by tradition from your fathers, [19] but with the precious blood of Christ, as of a lamb without blemish and without spot. [20] He indeed was foreordained before the foundation of the world, but was manifest in these last times for you.

2 Corinthians 4:18-19: Now all things are of God, who has reconciled us to Himself through Jesus Christ, and has given us the ministry of reconciliation, [19] that is, that God was in Christ reconciling the world to Himself, not imputing their trespasses to them, and has committed to us the word of reconciliation.

Without this reconciliation with His God, the man is a sitting duck for deception and seduction by Satan, who virtually steels or kills his worship by keeping him away from God, the church and true spirituality. Man's sexuality by itself becomes his own snare, in the absence of his real stronghold, his worship. Indeed, the thing that you were born for is what you do best and you can hardly be defeated in it; that is the power of the worship of the male man.

Men Must Fight Back

Men must recognize the wheeling and dealing of Satan, and fight back. We must be clear about our basic identity—an integration of our sexuality and our worship. We must fulfil our leadership role as men. We cannot afford to accept arbitrary definitions of who we are. In order to rediscover who we really are, we must come back to the worship of our Creator as we were designed to do, and restore the necessary balance to our lives. We must come back to our homes and be the guards, guides and governors of our households, providing the safety, security and love that our wives and children need. We must make sure that we empower our sons and properly father our daughters. We must love our wives as Christ loved the Church and gave Himself for her (Eph. 5:25). In so doing we will restore normalcy in family life and by extension in society as a whole.

On the other hand, women must begin to intercede for their men, both their husbands and their sons. Do not curse them. Women, you should understand that your men, being the legally designated heads of your homes and our society as a whole, are chief targets for Satan. His aim is to steal, kill and destroy. All women should be aware that society is as strong as its men, and should seek to support their men rather than fight them. God is the real game-changer; He can change the man if you call on Him. He is the initiator and designer of marriage, and like a new Rolls Royce, the manufacturer must be consulted if anything goes wrong. One does not take a Rolls Royce to a roadside mechanic for repairs.

9

ASSUMED GENDER TYPES AND INEVITABLE CONSEQUENCES

There is an increasing trend in which many people, including young children, claim to have varied degrees of deep feelings contrary to what their anatomy, sexual organs, internal hormonal composition or their DNA would suggest. Some are said to be frustrated with their original sexual designation to the point of cross-dressing, altering their sexual genitalia and acting in an opposite sexual capacity to what is indicated by their biological make up. Many would often accentuate their walk or speech to reflect what they claim to feel internally. Some would even make drastic surgical changes to their facial or bodily features, as well as ingest an abundance of the dominant hormones of the opposite sex in order to manifest the traits of that other sex. The latter are more commonly described as transsexuals. [88]

Still others may not necessarily show outward signs as afore mentioned, yet would harbour deep sexual feelings for the same-sex (gays [men and boys] and lesbians [women and girls]) as well as both sexes (bisexual). Most of these feelings would translate into corresponding sexual acts, backed up by

---
[88] Various online sources

legal claims for same-sex marriage. Many have also identified a "third sex," apart from male and female, known as "intersex." The latter are those who are said to be born with abnormal sexual features, be it genitals, hormones, chromosomes, malformed or absent gonads. [89]

Then there are those who pride themselves as "queer" owing to their general orientation to same-sex rather than the normal heterosexual feelings and practice. Yet another category of this gender melee is "questioning." These are those who are said to have not yet quite made up their minds regarding their sexual preference or orientation. Still another is "pansexuals"—those who are attracted to all sexes and "genders." Then there are the "asexuals," owing to the absence of sexual feelings. Some have also identified "allies" (or mere supporters) as a gender category.[90] That makes for the acronym LGBTQQIPAA

Still further, there are many who have felt that their particular sexual orientation has been omitted from the foregoing list and should be included. Thus, another school of thought is to use instead the acronym LGBTQQIP2SAA so as to include a category called "two spirit."[91] The fact is that once gender is lifted from sex and made out to be a social construct, the above phenomenon is the inevitable result—a long chain of sexual enigmas. All restrictions are removed, and therefore the concept of gender can be used to fit anybody's fancy.

Gender as a Social Construct Ressembles Biblical Eisegesis

Yes, indeed, this fallacy is equivalent to the phenomenon of eisegesis (normally applied to theological studies), in which extraneous materials outside of the biblical text are introduced in an attempt to explain the biblical passage.

---

[89] Ibid.
[90] Ibid
[91] Ibid.

Eisegesis is the process of interpreting a text or portion of text in such a way that the process introduces one's own presuppositions, agendas, or biases into and onto the text. This is commonly referred to as reading into the text.[92]

Eisegesis is one of the enemies of sound biblical exegesis (the unearthing of the original meaning of the biblical text). It is a slap in the face of rational and prudent thought to simply redefine a term from a purely subjective standpoint. Thus, the attempt to redefine gender is overwhelmingly a case of literary "eisegesis." The word is basically forced to mean what it never meant and could never mean by virtue of its etymology. By lifting gender from sex as its base and forcing it to mean what they claim it means, they have effectively imposed "a preconceived or foreign meaning" to the term.[93] As we mentioned in an earlier chapter, the advocates of same-sex unions and other forms of sexual perversions rest their case on a circular logic, a literary fallacy. What is more ludicrous is that these baseless assumptions are now being used to alter human culture, the home, family life and society at large.

How can sane-thinking and God-fearing people all sit by and say nothing in defence of truth? Young people are going to the dictionary now and seeing for the first time what we know are redefinitions of certain terms. They are sitting in primary, secondary and tertiary educational institutions and unquestionably accepting concocted substitutes for the definition of critical terminologies, having no idea of the original or correct meaning. What a debacle now facing the human race!

All are being forced to drink the cup of falsification as if it is the authentic and original brew. The call to every God-fearing

---

[92] Wikipedia, s.v. Exegesis
[93] Believe the Sign, s.v., eisegesis. http://en.believethesign.com/index.php/Eisegesis.

man or woman, boy and girl is to rise up and speak the truth to save civilization, or else within a few years, with all this focus on same-sex and the associated gender confusion, the human race could gradually become extinct, God forbid.

Paul's Prognosis of Today's Gender Crisis (Warning from the Book of Romans)

Please recall that I raised this issue in the introductory chapter. In the book of Romans, chapter 1, verses 18 to 32, the Apostle Paul, some two thousand years ago, did a perfect future analysis of life in the 21st century. He sent out a warning to all those who would regard God with contempt and ignore His truth and precepts. He begins by stating emphatically:

> For the wrath of God is revealed from heaven against all ungodliness and unrighteousness of men, who suppress the truth in unrighteousness, because what may be known of God is manifest in them, for God has shown it to them (vv. 18-19).

Those who smother the truth by their unrighteous living are earmarked for God's judgment, because they do it deliberately, being fully aware of who God is and what He demands of them. All the essential factors for believing that God is real have been revealed within them by way of their human spirit, which actually originated from God. God does not necessarily have to go out of His way to show them; He speaks from within and expects that each person would respond to that inner voice. So, there is an internal witness to the realty of God in every man.

Then Paul points to the external witness for the substantiality of God:

> For since the creation of the world His invisible attributes are clearly seen, being understood by the things that are made, even His eternal power and Godhead, so that they are without excuse (v. 20).

God's invisibility does not diminish His reality as God, for nature is the canvas on which He has painted "live pictures," reflecting His supernatural attributes. So that there are two major scripts that reflect God's reality—(i) the word of God (the Holy Bible), which reveals His creative, restorative and reconciliatory capacity and power; and (ii) nature, which is His masterpiece "live" portrait of who He is. The psalmist confirms this:

> The heavens declare the glory of God; and the firmament shows His handiwork. Day unto day utters speech, and night unto night reveals knowledge. There is no speech nor language where their voice is not heard. Their line has gone out through all the earth, and their words to the end of the world (Ps. 19:1-4).

Paul concludes that because of both the internal and external witnesses to the reality of God, no man is excusable, whether he is atheist, homosexual, agnostic, new age thinker, sceptic, or even devil-worshipper.

Paul is not merely assuming but is emphatic that every man knows God; notwithstanding, there are those who deliberately choose not to glorify Him as God:

> because, although they knew God, they did not glorify Him as God, nor were thankful, but became futile in their thoughts, and their foolish hearts were darkened (Rom. 1:21).

In his prognosis of man's last-day rebellion and its dire consequences, the Apostle uses the prophetic perfect tense (effectively a past tense to express the surety of the future event). He does this so as to leave no doubt whatsoever that this would be the state of affairs in these days. Unregenerate man simply chooses to be ungrateful and ignore God and His established standard for his or her life. As a result, such a person becomes numbered among the foolish in the eyes of God and his very heart becomes darkened, unable to be even convicted by his wrong deeds.

Thus, "professing to be wise, they became fools" (v. 22). What a catastrophic outcome! Those who think they are wise and would try to use their worldly wisdom to outmode God and His standard of righteousness end up to be fools, "for the fool has said in his heart that 'there is no God' (Ps. 14:1). The Bible clearly states: "For the wisdom of this world is foolishness with God. For it is written, 'He catches the wise in their own craftiness'" (1 Cor. 3:19). Moreover, the Apostle (in 1 Cor. 2:6-8) again makes it clear to us where the so-called wisdom of this world lies in contrast to God's wisdom, and that of His Church:

> However, we speak wisdom among those who are mature, yet not the wisdom of this age, nor of the rulers of this age, who are coming to nothing. But we speak the wisdom of God in a mystery, the hidden wisdom which God ordained before the ages for our glory, which none of the rulers of this age knew; for had they known, they would not have crucified the Lord of glory.

Paul continues his prognosis by implying that in their brain-restricted, earthly "wisdom" or rather their "smartness," or in reality, their folly, the post-modern sceptics

> changed the glory of the incorruptible God into an image made like corruptible man—and birds and four-footed animals and creeping things (Rom. 1:23).

In other words, they engaged in reductionism of the Divine precepts, belittling the image of God, the Creator and Lord of the universe. It was a deliberate act on their part to virtually make themselves "God" in changing His moral and ethical standards into corrupt and animalistic practices. What a grave human tragedy!

As a result,

> God also gave them up to uncleanness, in the lusts of their hearts, to dishonor their bodies among themselves, who

exchanged the truth of God for the lie, and worshiped and served the creature rather than the Creator, who is blessed forever. Amen (vv. 24-25)

How accurate is the Apostle Paul! He saw this clear picture of 21st century contemporary society over two thousand years ago. What he outlined is exactly what is happening now. As pointed out earlier, our diagnosis of this present human dilemma is made so much easier by Paul's prognosis.

Paul continues:

For this reason God gave them up to vile passions. For even their women exchanged the natural use for what is against nature. Likewise also the men, leaving the natural use of the woman, burned in their lust for one another, men with men committing what is shameful, and receiving in themselves the penalty of their error which was due (vv. 26, 27).

Here is the cruncher. God demands honour and respect for His creative power and authority. Wherever this is not forthcoming, He reserves the right to reject those who calculatingly and habitually spurn His righteousness as well as his moral and ethical standards. God gives up such individuals to vile passions [*pathe atimias* (Gk)] or "passions of dishonour." The feelings operating within such individuals are "against nature" and not true love; it is lust (or inordinate or unethical affections) and is dishonourable in the sight of God.

Consequently, those who spurn the authority of God for their own standard of righteousness find themselves forsaking the natural use of the opposite sex and gravitating to "passions of dishonour" for the same-sex. The Bible considers this abnormal affection and practice as *"shameful,"* and deserving *"the penalty of their error which was due."*

According to Apostle Paul, these passions of dishonour

gradually deteriorate to a "debased mind," where people do

> those things which are not fitting; [29] being filled with all unrighteousness, sexual immorality, wickedness, covetousness, maliciousness, full of envy, murder, strife, deceit, evil-mindedness; they are whisperers, [30] backbiters, haters of God, violent, proud, boasters, inventors of evil things, disobedient to parents, undiscerning, untrustworthy, unloving, unforgiving, unmerciful; [32] who knowing the righteous judgment of God, that those who practice such things are deserving of death, not only do the same but also approve of those who practice them.

Look at verse 32; this prognosis by Paul, the Apostle, is so accurate that it even identifies what the LBGT community now calls "allies," that is, people who approve and fully support their cause, although not engaged in such practices themselves. Wow! Should there be any further proof that the Bible is the unadulterated Word of God?

Violating the Levitical Code

The Levitical code in Numbers 18 calls same-sex behaviour "an abomination" and "perversion":

> [22.]You shall not lie with a male as with a woman. It is an abomination. [23] Nor shall you mate with any animal, to defile yourself with it. Nor shall any woman stand before an animal to mate with it. It is perversion. [24] Do not defile yourselves with any of these things; for by all these the nations are defiled, which I am casting out before you.

The Bible states clearly here, as we saw in Romans chapter 1, that homosexuality is forbidden by God as well as all forms of sexual perversion, including bestiality. There is no room for compromise here. Some may argue that this Levitical code is archaic and not presently applicable. One does not have to be versed in rocket science to see its application to today's society. This is universal truth, applicable to all eras of history and all human cultures. A nation becomes polluted when its people practice the identified abominable acts, together with other sins of the Levitical code; God also regards that nation as an outcast before Him.

The Levitical code continues:

> [25]For the land is defiled; therefore I visit the punishment of its iniquity upon it, and the land vomits out its inhabitants. [26] You shall therefore keep My statutes and My judgments, and shall not commit any of these abominations, either any of your own nation or any stranger who dwells among you [27] (for all these abominations the men of the land have done, who were before you, and thus the land is defiled), [28] lest the land vomit you out also when you defile it, as it vomited out the nations that were before you.

God, in the foregoing verses, reveals to us that because the land is defiled, He visits the penalty of its iniquity upon it, meaning that there is a scorpion tail effect linked to all-out rebellion against God's precepts. Whereas one may feel that it is within one's rights to do whatever one may desire, the scorpion tail always lashes back and virtually generates a self-destructive impact. In other words, the evil that men do strikes back like a boomerang, with devastating consequences. The land ultimately vomits out its inhabitants.

The foregoing may well be why several nations that give way to lasciviousness and sexual pollution experience such high levels of suicide, violence and murders, or even natural disasters. Many pride themselves in abandonment to the flesh and practice all forms of vulgarity, befouling the dignity of the human person, and reaping heavily the consequences of such.

God warns all of us that if we commit these abominations, the land, reeling under the weight of sinful pollution, perversion and curses, would spew us out also. This is how many nations have deteriorated, resulting in great nests of evil works, destruction and death. On the other hand, God advises us in Proverbs chapter 14 and verse 34: "Righteousness exalts a nation, but sin is a reproach to any people."

10

THE DISCRIMINATION SMOKESCREEN

The concept of discrimination has been largely abused, and employed as a fiercely biased tool by the social scientists and other advocates of gender fluidity. In reality, the word discrimination has several nuances, many of them very positive in nature. Notwithstanding, there seems to be an agenda to whittle down the notion of discrimination to one meaning and one meaning only: "the practice of unfairly treating a person or group of people differently from other people or groups of people."[94] All other applications of this word are basically ignored to the point where any form of critical analysis done on certain beliefs and practices is deemed as unfair treatment; it does not matter whether the critical action contributes to the welfare of society or not.

Analysis of Discrimination

According to the Online Etymology Dictionary, the word "discriminate" is a derivative of the Latin *discriminatus* and *discernere*, meaning to divide, separate, distinguish, set apart, discern, perceive, or even sift.[95] Thus, discrimination must also

---

[94] Merriam-Webster online
[95] Online Etymology Dictionary, s.v. *discriminate*

allow for making distinctions between things of good quality as opposed to things of bad quality. One should be allowed to mark the difference between right and wrong without being accused of prejudice against or dislike or even hate for the person practicing what one perceives to be wrong.

For example, it would be ideal for a good parent to advise his or her son to stay away or separate himself from bad company. Can one claim that that parent is discriminating against the son for doing so? It would be pointless for a good parent to be so accused. In the same way, it is absurd to label a person as discriminating against another if the former identifies the bad qualities of certain sexual behaviours, and cautions about their possible dangers to individuals, families and society at large.

Indeed, discrimination is a problem when a person makes "invidious distinctions prejudicial to a class of persons (usually based on race or colour").[96] To be labelled as unfairness or injustice, discrimination must show unfavourable treatment of someone who says or does the same thing that another person says or does but treated favourably. It cannot be unfair if one points out objectively that despite the race, colour, creed or minority group to which a person belongs, there are certain practices that are unnatural, unwholesome and detrimental to the well-being of the individual, other persons, the family structure as well as future civilization.

The foregoing type of discrimination has nothing to do with a particular social group or class; one is dealing with universal truths here, aligned with nature as the truth maker. Thus, misdemeanours run across the board, regardless of the private notions of a particular social group. The laws of nature are rules by which life should be lived in order to ensure that the human race does not plunge into irreversible anarchy, self-destruction and even extinction. If one points out to another the dangers of violating such laws, how can that be an act of unfair treatment towards another?

---

[96] Ibid.

To be more exact, there seems to be a desperate effort to protect certain behaviours that society would have frowned upon in previous times. Thus, there has been a deliberate attempt by the sociologists, feminist movement and the LBGT community to adopt a myopic view of discrimination. Conveniently, as long as one voices disagreement with a particular sexual practice, whether on the basis of conscience or by way of the hard sciences (physics, chemistry, biology), the objector is immediately branded as discriminating against the person or persons engaged in the respective practice. This is unjust and hypocritical.

The subtlety of making "gender" a social construct is to cater for the legitimacy of social groups like the LBGT community. Once that legitimacy could be established then the rest of society could be easily accused of discriminating against the said social groups because of their gender[s]. Once the rest of society disagrees with their set standard, we are accused of discrimination, notwithstanding that both their concept of "gender" and the social communities so conceived are unnatural by any stretch of the imagination and largely self-created. "Legitimacy" is left hanging in the air, so to speak. Thus the discrimination claim by same-sex advocates is totally unfounded and predominantly subjective.

Reverse Discrimination

Ironically, the overemphasis on discrimination claims by a particular community while at the same time ignoring the rights of the rest of society is itself a form of discrimination known as "reverse discrimination," which, according to Cambridge Dictionary, is defined as

> The act of giving advantage to those groups in society that are often treated unfairly, usually because of their race, sex,

or sexuality.[97]

So that, one has to be wary of the phenomenon that even in the attempt to accuse others of discrimination, the complainant could well be practicing a form of negative discrimination or reverse discrimination. This is especially the case when one fails to see that there are also neutral or even positive connotations attached to the notion of discrimination, and that it is not all blatantly prejudicial.

Varied Sources

The Merriam-Webster dictionary defines the word discriminate to mean: (i) "to make a difference in treatment or favour on a basis other than individual merit"; (ii) "to mark or perceive the distinguishing or peculiar features of something"; (iii) "to distinguish, differentiate, or discern"; (iv) "perception, insight and acumen or 'the power to see what is not evident to the average mind,' or the power to distinguish and select what is true or appropriate or excellent."[98] This source also makes a very important observation:

> Although many methods or motives for discriminating are unfair and undesirable (or even illegal), the verb itself has a neutral history.[99]

This statement belies the bias by modern-day thinkers that discrimination is always to be seen in a negative or destructive sense. Present-day intellectuals have smothered all flexibility associated with the word, so that there is no breathing space, so to speak, for anyone to discern that which is fitting or even inappropriate based on moral, ethical or spiritual criteria or the

---

[97] Cambridge Dictionary. https://dictionary.cambridge.org/dictionary/english/discrimination
[98] Miriam Webster, s.v. discrimate
[99] Ibid.

dictates of one's conscience. There seems to be a concerted effort to screen off or smother that which is true, appropriate or excellent from that which is self-made, convenient but unwholesome, debased and destructive. As we discovered earlier, that too is a form of unwelcomed discrimination.

The online English Oxford Living Dictionaries show discrimination as (i) "unjust or prejudicial treatment of different categories of people, especially on the grounds of race, age or sex"; (ii) "the recognition and understanding of the difference between one thing and another, for example being able to distinguish between right and wrong"; (iii) "the ability to judge what is of high quality; good judgment or taste."[100] As long as one ignores the notions of distinguishing right from wrong or the right to exercise one's ability to judge what is of high quality or of low quality, one would always see discrimination in a myopic manner. One would always judge any form of critical distinction as unjust or prejudicial. Such a view is underpinned by intellectual dishonesty and social bias.

Intellectuals have so stripped the word discrimination from its other nuances that the very mention of the word tends to conjure up in people's minds that something negative and unfair is intended. Indeed, it is a matter of intellectual dishonesty for one to be aware of the various nuances and applications of the word "discriminate" and yet restrict every reference to the word as treating one unfairly. Certainly, one of the reasons why the laws of governments around the world have upheld measures like the buggery law and other sexual prohibitions is because such laws identify with the good-making quality of "discrimination." That is, such laws recognize the difference between things that are of good quality and those that are not and seek to safeguard a nation and a people from destroying themselves.

Have some human rights advocates become so blind-sided by their resistance to God's divine order that they can no longer discern the difference between things that are of

---
[100] English Oxford Living Dictionaries (online)

good quality and those that are not? To use the law merely to protect a deep feeling towards a particular sex or sexual practice (sexual orientation), oblivious of moral considerations, becomes incredulous, if at the same time, the law does not protect the driving or compelling "deep feelings" of the paedophile, the serial killer, the thief, or even the murderer. That's how awkward the law could become when it tries to embrace wrong, setting off a domino effect of violations of truth, including nature itself, and reaping dire consequences in the process. As a result, the law finds itself being constrained to suspend standard prohibitions necessary for the progress of a civil society, and give way to lasciviousness and unharnessed, even deadly, passions and practices.

Put another way, wouldn't the law be discriminating against many convicted criminals or murderers if it shows unbridled sympathy to the "deep feelings" of the LBGTIQ community, yet at the same time holds in contempt the "deep feelings" of myriads of offenders? Many would vehemently, but hypocritically so, argue against this notion on the basis that the law is there to ensure that those practices that are "wrong" should be punishable by whatever measures the law sees fit to use. After all, the law makes critical decisions for the benefit of society, one may argue. Then, why should violations of standard morality such as LBGTIQ practices not be treated in the same way and judged for their bad-making quality, since they are contrary to nature, and thus not true human rights? Moreover, many such practices have been scientifically judged to be unhygienic and unhealthy.

What are Human Rights?

Human rights are inalienable rights, rights which naturally accrue to us as human beings. Here is a definition from the United Nations:

> Human rights are rights inherent to all human beings, whatever our nationality,

place of residence, sex, national or ethnic origin, colour, religion, language, or any other status. We are all equally entitled to our human rights without discrimination. These rights are all interrelated, interdependent and indivisible.[101]

Critically, this writer questions the inclusion of the phrase "or any other status" in the above definition, in light of the absence of specific reference to "nature" as an important qualifier for determining such a category. One may argue that the word "inherent" should be adequate to take care of that objection. Notwithstanding, the idea of "inherent" does not necessarily mean "natural"; it may simply mean "that which is handed down," suggesting that even an unnatural practice could eventually be considered inherent. Thus it makes room for contrived categories such as "sexual orientation" and "sexual preference."

This writer prefers the following definition by BusinessDictionary:

> The fundamental rights that humans have by the fact of being human, and that are neither created nor can be abrogated by any government.[102]

The crucial point in the above definition is "by the fact of being human." The fact of being human speaks of all the natural attributes of humanness that can neither be created (or re-created) nor abrogated (rescinded, invalidated, nullified or dissolved) by any earthly authority. That is true human rights—a purely natural claim or entitlement. It would then be inappropriate

---

[101] "What are Human Rights"; United Nations Human Rights, Office of the High Commissioner.
[102] http://www.businessdictionary.com/definititon/human-rights.html.

for one to appeal to human rights to cover notions or behaviours that contravene the laws and norms of nature.

Going back to the UN definition above, indeed all true human rights are said to be *universal* in that we all as human beings have the same rights since they are naturally accruing. Human rights are also *interrelated* in that one person's rights cannot strike down another person's and vice versa, since they are all natural and reflect nature's orderliness. Furthermore, human rights are *interdependent*, suggesting that they are only authentic when they do not stand in isolation of normal human needs as established by our Creator. Being *inalienable*, they should not be denied unless they fail to adhere to natural and civil laws as well as moral and spiritual values.[103] They should be respected everywhere. Finally, the *indivisibility* of human rights suggests that whether one's rights "relate to civil, cultural, economic, political or social issues, human rights are inherent to the dignity of every human person."[104]

The big question is whether or not one is dealing with an authentic human right every time one appeals to the protective covering of "human rights." First of all, since human rights are naturally accruing, they cannot evolve over time to match mere human imaginations or fancies, as modern day secular scholars want us to believe. Human rights must be based on "what is already there"—the established laws of nature, not on behavioural intrusions contrary to God's creative order, begging for human law to cover them. Truth is not convenience and neither are authentic human rights.

Indeed, present-day lawmakers are double-faulting by first employing a myopic view of "discrimination," restricted only to "unjust or prejudicial treatment of different categories of people, especially on the grounds of race, age or sex"; that is, no other nuance is allowable. Second, they accept as "human

---
[103] Various online sources.
[104] Human Rights Principles; United Nations Popular Fund (UNFPA) https://www.unfpa.org/resources/human-rights-principles

rights" every imagination of the human heart, however deviant, abnormal, queer or counterproductive. This writer sees this as grave intellectual manipulation, and properly put, devaluation of true "human rights." The truth is that the overwhelming quest for pleasure and the failure to discern purpose have landed modern society into this endless landscape of sexual fantasies—from L to G to LGBTIQQIP2SAA, to God knows where else.

The intellectual smokescreen seems deliberate. Supreme court judges, presidents, legal framers are all imposing their "power ethics" or "mightism," championed by Plato and other Greek philosophers, which says in essence: *What is right or just is nothing but the interest of the stronger.*[105] In other words, "x is good once those who have power in the community say x is good." This philosophy totally ignores the fact that true ethics deal with prescription (what we should be doing) and not merely description (what is in fact being done).

As pointed out earlier, postmodern society's loose, but conveniently coined application of "discrimination" masks one's natural human rights to discern or "recognize the difference between things that are of good quality and those that are not" (positive discrimination). How could human society that hopes to advance or even survive build laws on that which is inauthentic? What a travesty! Thank God He is still the righteous and final Judge.

---

[105] "Power Ethics-Thesis #9 Power Ethics claim that might is..." https://www.coursehero.com/file/17711506/Power-Ethics/ .

11

WHAT THEN IS THE PURPOSE OF THE LAW?

The law was primarily designed to protect truth, morality (i.e., distinction between right and wrong) and ethics (moral principles and practices), and in the process, correct wrong and preserve integrity so that human dignity, rights and liberties are upheld and societal stability is safeguarded. Put another way, the law was meant to safeguard society from self-destructing. The Holy Bible tells what the purpose of the law is, which should be no different in principle to how law should serve our contemporary society: "What purpose then does the law serve? It was added because of transgressions..." (Galatians 3:19).

God introduced the law to prevent violation of His unchanging standard of truth and morality, essential for the stability and well-being of any society. Secular governments later adopted most of these moral principles for guiding their societies. This seems to be one of the overwhelming reasons why the original framers of the constitutions of several nations, including my nation, the Republic of Trinidad and Tobago (T&T), referenced the principles of the "Supremacy of God" in the preamble of their constitution. In the same token, much is also made of the dignity of the human person as well as moral and spiritual values and the rule of law. Hereunder is a sample of the preamble of the constitution of the Republic of Trinidad and Tobago:

Whereas, the people of Trinidad and Tobago—

> (a) have affirmed that the Nation of Trinidad and Tobago is founded upon principles that acknowledge the supremacy of God, faith in fundamental human rights and freedoms, the position of the family in a society of free men and free institutions, the dignity of the human person and the equal and inalienable rights with which all members of the human family are endowed by their Creator...[106]

The framers then ensured that by adding a limiting clause, they properly contextualized "free men" and "free institutions" referred to above:

> Clause (d): recognise that men and institutions remain free only when freedom is founded upon respect for moral and spiritual values and the rule of law...[107]

The law then must not appear to be dragged into a fool's paradise, accommodating all forms of wrong when it was designed to protect truth, morality and ethics in the first place and ultimately maintain integrity and stability of society.

Moreover, if one divorces morality from law, as some of our modern lawmakers suggest, one would be treating law as if it were superior to morality and not a companion of it. This is a

---

[106] The Constitution of the Republic of Trinidad and Tobago, Preamble.
[107] Ibid.

formula for a chaotic and disordered society with minimal moral or ethical boundaries, ultimately becoming lawless and devoid of wholesome or good-making qualities. This would be opposite to what the law was intended to uphold. A state of anarchy or the rule of the jungle, so to speak, would be the logical consequence.

Sir William Blackstone, an eighteenth century English jurist judge and Tory politician, in discussing natural law, sees the law of nature as "dictated by God Himself" and "superior in obligation to any other."[108] Blackstone continues:

> no human laws are of any validity, if contrary to this; and such of them as are valid derive all their force, and all their authority, mediately or immediately, from this original.[109]

He quips further that had man's reasoning remained as pristine as it was before the fall, "we should need no other guide but this."[110] However, man's reason is now corrupt "and his understanding full of ignorance and error."[111] This has warranted, according to Blackstone, divine intervention in the form of the revealed law as outlined in the Holy Scriptures, which *are found upon comparison to be really a part of the original law of nature.*"[112]

I find Blackstone's insights to be extremely profound. I have always held the belief (my perception drawn mainly from the Holy Scriptures) that man was originally designed to live by his conscience, which by nature is linked to God, God Himself having breathed His breath into man. Conscience is the heart of man's spirit, which became estranged from God with the fall of

---

[108] "Natural Law and Sir William Blackstone." All About Philosophy. https://www.allaboutphilosophy.org/natural-law-and-sir-william-blackstone-faq.htm
[109] Ibid.
[110] Ibid.
[111] Ibid.
[112] Ibid.

man, but is reconnected to God via salvation and the born-again experience through Jesus Christ. Look at these scriptural verses:

> 1 Pet. 1:18-20: Knowing that you were not redeemed with corruptible things, like silver or gold, from your aimless conduct received by the tradition from your fathers, [19]but with the precious blood of Christ, as of a lamb without blemish and without spot. [20] He indeed was foreordained before the foundation of the world, but was manifest in these last times for you

> 2 Cor. 5:18-19: Now all things are of God, who has reconciled us to Himself through Jesus Christ, and has given us the ministry of reconciliation, [19]that is, that God was in Christ reconciling the world to Himself, not [a]imputing their trespasses to them, and has committed to us the word of reconciliation; and

> Romans 9:1: I tell the truth in Christ, I am not lying, my conscience also bearing me witness in the Holy Spirit

Conscience is the primary faculty of man's being. Man is trichotomous, comprising of body, soul and spirit. Whereas, his body was formed from the dust of the ground (or red earth), man's spirit came directly from God via the act of inbreathing.

Now, God is by nature spirit, according to John 4:24. So, when God breathed into man's nostril the breath (*nishmat*) or spirit of life in Genesis 2:7, God in effect gave man part of Himself. It is that "spirit" component which we must use to worship the Father in spirit and in truth, as Jesus tells us in John 4:23-24.

Recall that in Romans chapter 1 and verse 19, Paul the Apostle reveals the nature of man's conscience when he says: "because what may be known of God is manifest in them, for God has shown it to them." How is it possible for that which may be known of God to be manifested in the human being, whether or not he is a born-again believer? The answer is: "through man's conscience"—the internal witness of the reality of God in man. The Apostle Paul strongly affirms this in Gal. 5:16-17:

> I say then: Walk in the Spirit, and you shall not fulfill the lust of the flesh. For the flesh lusts against the Spirit, and the Spirit against the flesh; and these are contrary to one another, so that you do not do the things that you wish.

Paul sees conscience speaking deep from the inside of each person, expressing what one truly wishes to do and thus, what God Himself ultimately desires. That is, conscience, by virtue of its origin, is prompting one to do only that which is in congruence with God's will. Yes, the things that we really want to do are lodged in our spirits, since the human spirit is of the same nature as God. Thus, there is a deep-seated desire in every man to do right, but the suppressive tendency within him is overwhelming because of the fall. For the same reason, man's conscience has been smothered or suppressed by the works of the flesh. Conscience is present but not acute or prominent (Rom. 1:18), and therefore, by itself, cannot provide adequate guidance for fallen man.

This is the reason why the Holy Spirit has been given to us, so that He could help us remove the shroud of darkness and allow the brightness of the light of His glory to shine deep into our souls. In the Spirit, we would no longer stumble and grope in the dark, but shall have the light of lights to guide us. The Holy Spirit will remove the bitter inner struggle between our flesh and our spirit and lift us out of the stronghold or jurisdiction of Satan. If one walks in the Spirit then the inferior flesh cannot smother or overcome the conscience, since the latter is spiritual in orientation.

Thus, the law is not really necessary for those who are led by the Spirit of the Lord since, all things being equal, such persons, by nature, would be in congruence with God's natural and revealed law. The Apostle makes the point quite succinctly in Romans 8:1-2:

> There is therefore now no condemnation to those who are in Christ Jesus, who do not walk according to the flesh, but according to the Spirit. ² For the law of the Spirit of life in Christ Jesus has made me free from the law of sin and death.

If I am living genuinely in Christ Jesus, the law that is designed to deal with sin and death could not condemn me, since being in Christ allows me to be governed by the higher law of the Spirit of life in Christ Jesus. The latter allows me to surpass all the demands of the lower law and automatically fulfil it. Once I am walking in the Spirit, I am living above the dictates of the flesh; thus there is no need for the lower law to police me. As a born again believer, the lower law does not govern my lifestyle anymore, but the superior "law of the Spirit of life in Christ Jesus" does.

The Apostle Paul drives home the point even further in 1 Timothy 1:9-10:

> Knowing this, that the law is not made for a righteous man, but for the lawless and disobedient, for the ungodly and for sinners, for unholy and profane, for murderers of fathers and murderers of mothers, for manslayers, for whoremongers, for them that defile themselves with mankind, for menstealers, for liars, for perjured persons, and if there be any other thing that is contrary to sound doctrine.

The combination of a God-oriented conscience (man's internal core nature) and man's external natural environment makes the reality of God undeniable, if man is willing to admit. Man's understanding of right and wrong, therefore, should be very clear, even without the revealed or written law.

Paul goes further and reiterates the reality of God from the standpoint of man's conscience in Rom. 2:12-15:

> For as many as have sinned without the law will also perish without law, and as many as have sinned in the law will be judged by the law [13] (for not the hearers of the law are just in the sight of God, but the doers of the law will be justified; [14] for when Gentiles, who do not have the law, by nature do the things in the law, these, although not having the law, are a law to themselves, [15] who show the work of the law written in their hearts, their conscience also bearing witness, and between themselves their thoughts accusing or else excusing them).

The point is reiterated that man's conscience speaks on behalf of God from the inside of his being; pointing out to us that there is an obligation to recognize the supremacy of God. So, for example, a man who grows up in the Amazon forest or the Himalaya Mountains and never heard the gospel preached would be judged on the basis of how he responded to the inner revelation of his conscience and the outer revelation of nature. The Scripture rightly says:

> The heavens declare the glory of God and the firmament shows His handiwork. Day unto day utters speech, and night unto night reveals knowledge (Ps. 19:1).

According to verse 15 of Romans chapter 2 (above), one's conscience would at first convict or accuse one of sin. If over a period of time, that conviction goes unheeded, that same conscience would simply begin to excuse that person, but with dire consequences. The conscience would gradually become insensitive to sin or its consequences until it becomes "seared with a hot iron," rendering that person a reprobate (1 Tim. 4:2; 2 Tim. 3:8; Rom. 1:28).

The Merriam-Webster gives us a secular definition of conscience, but it links right back to morality:

> the sense or consciousness of the moral

goodness or blameworthiness of one's own conduct, intentions, or character together with a feeling of obligation to do right or be good.

The problem in man is his corrupt Adamic nature which he cannot conquer with his depraved inner conscience. Thus, the signals emanating from his conscience are weak and are easily overridden until he smothers truth and his mind excuses him from wrongdoing. Indeed, without the power of the Holy Spirit, man's distorted conscience, ravaged by the forces of darkness, does not carry the overcoming power that is needed to combat wrong-doing. Yes, without God, man becomes a hapless victim of his own fleshly cravings and a sitting duck for satanic manipulations.

What man could no longer see through the eyes of conscience and even by way of nature, God had to write on tablets of stone, so that man would keep that which is written before his natural eyes as God's statutes and laws. These are the very laws that were originally "written" on man's conscience by our Master Creator Himself.

Thus the law was meant to provide the guidelines which man's warped conscience would have missed. It is really a back-up plan for the effective operation of man's conscience and not an end in itself. Lawmakers are at fault if they see the law as an end in itself and not a means to an end, or if they see the law as superior to morality and righteousness.

12

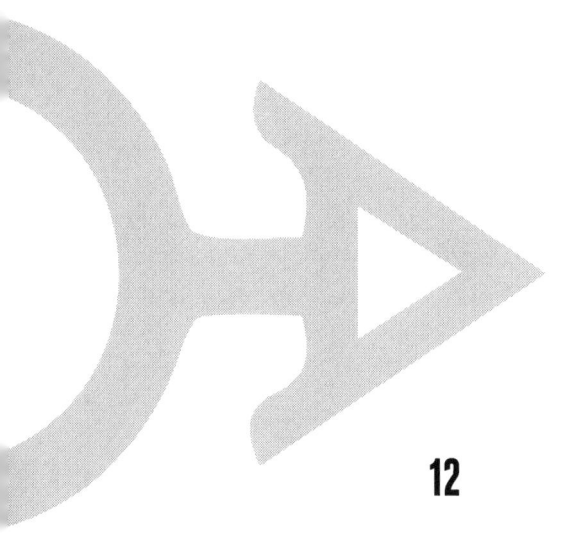

HOMOPHOBIA REALLY A CLEVER RED HERRING

The following is a newspaper article written by this writer and published by the Trinidad Guardian Newspaper, Trinidad, West Indies on Wednesday June 6th, 2011:[113]

I read with utter consternation an article entitled "New Politics Means Respect Rights of All," the editorial opinion of one of our leading daily newspapers, dated Friday 20th May 2011. It is difficult to believe and accept that moral standards have deteriorated that far within societies around the world and more so in the "responsible" media. In support of a recent march "to mark International Day Against Homophobia and Transphobia," held in a major capitol city by a "core activist group" on behalf of gays and transgenders, that editorial concluded: "The People's Partnership administration, and the Parliament, should fall in line with advancing world trends, turn the page on past obscurantist and homophobic attitudes and prejudices, and have the laws appropriately reflect progressive approaches of the present and future. That would indeed be new politics."

First of all, is the media to advocate the legitimizing of lifestyles clearly against God's creative order and design, and

---

[113] Joseph Duncan. Trinidad Guardian Newspaper, Viewpoint. June 6th, 2011.

to label all those who oppose this as obscurantist, homophobic and bigoted? Is this responsible behaviour? Do standard media ethics permit such promotion, especially when the majority of the population, including our precious young minds and tertiary scholars, are not of the same persuasion (as the said article admitted)? Secondly, can any ideology rooted in subjectivity and humanistic feelings be logically governed by civil Law, since civil Law itself presupposes objective truth? If there is no objective truth, why then are people jailed for doing wrong? What standard of wrong and right do the civil authorities use? Is the source merely Government, or the legal tradition? Who made the Law then? It certainly could not be subjective man, for every man is right in his own eyes. There has to be an indisputable Authority, a Master Creator, who set human purpose in motion and communicated to His highest creation the moral codes that would ensure the success of human civilization. That is objective truth.

How could one then speak of the need for Government to "fall in with advancing world trends ... and have the laws appropriately reflect progressive approaches of the present and future" when the reference is to blatant violations of God's creative order and design? Does progress now mean "popular wrong" rather than moral and ethical correctness, promoting family life as the Creator designed it? Is this progress just because the UN recommends it? Fortunately, there are still level-headed Governments and people around the world. Ugandan Minister of State for Ethics and Integrity, Dr. James Nsaba Buturo, vehemently objects to the UN's "surreptitious mission to impose acceptance of homosexuality on sovereign countries, affirming" that Uganda will not bow to international pressure to legalize 'abnormal practices'[114]. Kudos are in order for that Government.

God was very clear in His design (Genesis 1:27): "So God

---

[114] Thaddeus M. Baklinski: "Uganda Refuses to Bow to United Nations Pressure ..." Life Site News, April 6, 2009. https://www.lifesitenews.com/news/uganda-refuses-to-bow-to-united-nations-pressure-to-accept-homosexuality.

created man in His own image; in the image of God He created him; male and female He created them." Yes, indeed, He made them male (Hebrew "zakar" [sharp male organ (the phallus or penis)] to be a donor of seed; and female (Hebrew "nekevah [womb or opening)] to receive the seed, bring it into union with the ovum (egg), cause conception, incubate and develop the fetus, and finally release the young into the world.

How then can one be branded as homophobic if one adheres to the foregoing master design and reject practices that violate the same? It is ridiculous to even imagine this. Unknowing to many people, the word homophobia is very recent, and hardly rooted in foundational philosophical thought. The word was coined by clinical psychologist George Weinberg in his book "Society and the Healthy Homosexual," in 1971, in defence of the homosexual. It combines the Greek words phobia ("fear") and homo ("the same," the "homo" referring to the term "homosexual"). It is rooted in perception and not fact, holding that all opposition to homosexuality reflects some kind of psychological disorder. It is "part of the lexicon of gay theory and activism" and now seen (more so by the unsuspecting and passive thinker) as parallel to the societal ills of "racism" and "sexism."

But the parallelism is unfounded and misplaced; the true parallel to "racism" and "sexism" is "homosexuality" itself and not so-called homophobia. "Homophobia" is indeed a red herring, cleverly created to divert attention from the abominable practice of homosexuality. What a sad day for mankind if we are blinded and deceived by such subtle intellectualization!

Ironically, the word homophobia is more applicable to homosexuals themselves. In the words of George Weinberg: "The roots of homophobia are fear ... It is based on the preposterous notion that if you are like everybody else you will be safe, secure and happy. And in the extreme that if you are good, you won't die."[115] What is then even more preposterous is to

---

[115] George Weinberg, "Love is Conspirational, Deviant and Magical," interview by Raj Ayyar; GayToday.com, Nov. 2002. www.gaytoday.com/interview/110102in. asp

take a terminology coined in defence of a practice that is clearly against nature, and as a counter measure against internal fears and conviction of practising homosexuals themselves, and use it to label all forms of opposition to such ungodly and abnormal practice. All God-fearing people should reject such labelling. It is the sin that God denounces, not the person.

How could civil Governments make provisions in the law for such subjective and objectionable habits? What prevents some interest group on bestiality or paedophilia rising up tomorrow morning and demanding equal rights? Wouldn't the Government of the day be obligated to accommodate them as well? That's how nonsensical this whole "human rights" thing gets.

So Weinberg's psychological wit was very clear in his masterminding of a recently coined word originally intended to allay the fears of homosexuals, and shifting "the locus of the 'problem' from gay men and lesbians to heterosexuals' intolerance."[116] How clever!

In his book, *Society and the Healthy Homosexual*, Weinberg, in his desperate attempt to establish that all those who object to a homosexual lifestyle are abnormal mentally, says in his opening statement on "homophobia": *"I would never consider a patient healthy unless he had overcome his prejudice against homosexuality."*[117] He relegates all opposition to homosexual behaviour to "fear,"[118] ignoring all moral or spiritual considerations, or postures linked to one's nature and conscience. So what really is homophobia and where does it belong, or where is it applicable? You can judge for yourself.

---

[116] Gregory Herek, "The Father of 'Homophobia': George Wineberg (1929-2017)." Beyond Homophobia, a weblog about sexual orientation, prejudice, science and policy, Mar. 24, 2017. https://herek.net/blog/the-father-of-homophobia-george-weinberg-1929-2017/

[117] George Weinberg, Society and the healthy homosexual, 1972. p. 1. St. Martin's Press New York.

[118] George Weinberg, "Love is Conspirational, Deviant and Magical," interview by Raj Ayyar; GayToday.com www.gaytoday.com/interview/110102in.asp

13

IN DEFENCE OF THE FAITH

In this chapter, this author provides you, the reader, with an example of Christian apologetics—that is, how one can defend truth and morality in the face of contrary positions upheld by legal authorities of our day. Hereunder is this author's response to a recent legal decision handed down by the High Court of Trinidad and Tobago on the buggery law; which was adapted as an endorsed statement/petition of several Faith Based Organizations in Trinidad and Tobago, and submitted to the Office of the Attorney General for consideration. The reader will see many of the principles discussed in the foregoing pages applied to the case in point.

Initially, the document is regurgitated as was submitted; however, in the latter part of this presentation, some of the points that have already been made in this book are only summarized for the sake of providing the reader with full context. Nevertheless, it is considered to be an appropriate evangelical/full gospel response to a secular oriented court ruling:

"I take note of the decision recently handed down by the presiding Justice on the 12th day of April 2018, in which he declared that Sections 13 and 16 of the Sexual Offenses Act

(SOA) '*were unconstitutional, illegal, null, void, invalid and are of no effect to the extent that these laws criminalize any acts constituting consensual conduct between adults.*'[119]

I note further the final court order delivered on September 20th, 2018, in which the court ordered that Section 13 of the SOA be amended to show that *"buggery means sexual intercourse **without consent** per anum by a male person with a male person or by a male person with a female person."* According to the court, consensual sexual intercourse per anum by an adult male with another adult male, or an adult male with an adult female is not buggery and therefore not an offense. The court also decided that Section 16 of the SOA be altered to show that "serious indecency" does not apply to a husband and wife and consenting persons who are both 16 years of age or more.[120]

In light of the foregoing, I draw attention to the preamble of the Constitution of the Republic of Trinidad and Tobago which states in part:[121]

Whereas the People of Trinidad and Tobago—

A. (Clause {a}): have affirmed that the Nation of Trinidad and Tobago is founded upon principles that acknowledge the supremacy of God, faith in fundamental human rights and freedoms, the position of the family in a society of free men and free institutions, the dignity of the human person and the equal and inalienable rights with which all members of the human family are endowed by their

---

[119] In The Matter Of An Application For Constitutional Redress Under S.14 Of The Constitution Between Jason Jones and The Attorney General Of Trinidad And Tobago. April 12th, 2018, The Order, paragraph 176.1, p. 53. Claim No. CV2017-00720.

[120] In The Matter Of An Application For Constitutional Redress Under S.14 Of The Constitution Between Jason Jones and The Attorney General Of Trinidad And Tobago. Sept. 20th, 2018, The Order, paragraphs 29.1 and 29.2. Claim No. CV2017-00720.

[121] Constitution of the Republic of Trinidad and Tobago Act, Chapter 1:01 Act 4 of 1976. Laws of Trinidad and Tobago, Ministry of Legal Affairs. https://www.oas.org/dil/Constitution_of_the_of_Trinidad_Tobago_Act_Act.pdf

Creator;

B. (Clause {d}): recognise that men and institutions remain free only when freedom is founded upon respect for moral and spiritual values and the rule of law;

C. (Clause {e}). desire that their Constitution should enshrine the above-mentioned principles and beliefs and make provision for ensuring the protection in Trinidad and Tobago of fundamental human rights and freedoms.

In its argument, the court noted the following in paragraph 14 of the April 12th, 2018 hearing:

> This is not a case about religious and moral beliefs but is one about the inalienable rights of a citizen under the Republican Constitution of Trinidad and Tobago; any citizen; all citizens . . . about the dignity of the person and not about the will of the majority or any religious debate.

Based on the preamble of our Constitution, I wish to advance the following points:

1. As a concerned citizen of this nation, I am of the belief that the learned judge erred in disregarding the very founding principles of our Constitution—considering "inalienable rights of a citizen" without at the same time giving due attention to the principles of "religious and moral beliefs" as implied strongly in the preamble of our constitution. It is these moral and spiritual values that should form a fundamental matrix for legal deliberations in Trinidad and Tobago, particularly with regard to the issue in question—sexuality and human behaviour. What is more is that closer attention must be paid to Clause (d) of the preamble: "recognise

that men and institutions remain free only when freedom is founded upon respect for moral and spiritual values and the rule of law." Thus, according to the Constitution of the Republic of Trinidad and Tobago, "inalienable rights" can only be authentic if and only when they coincide with moral and spiritual values and the rule of law. Thus, a case for inalienable rights for any citizen of Trinidad and Tobago seems futile if those rights are not rooted in moral and spiritual values and the rule of law, as so strongly stipulated by our constitution.

2. I am convinced that the aforesaid "moral and spiritual values and the rule of law" are referenced in the context of the acknowledgement of the supremacy of God, and "the position of the family," as the Supreme God established it from the beginning where He created the human race male and female (Gen. 1:27), and then instituted marriage between them for establishing the family as the basic unit of society (Gen. 2:24): "Therefore a man shall leave his father and mother and be joined to his wife, and they shall become one flesh."

3. In the same token, according to the Preamble, reference to "the dignity of the human person" cannot be authentic unless the associated action or practice is aligned to "moral and spiritual values and the rule of law." Thus, we believe that by ignoring religious and moral factors in its judgment, the court would have been fallacious in citing "the dignity of the person" as a rationale for legitimizing sexual intercourse per anum. What constitutes dignity but the adherence to "moral and spiritual values and the rule of law" as clearly spelt out in the Preamble?

4. To exclude religious and moral beliefs from a legal matter concerning buggery in Trinidad and Tobago seems to be a violation of our inalienable rights to freedom of conscience and religious beliefs as Christians and other faith based organizations (FBOs); we represent over nine hundred

thousand (900,000) citizens of this land, whose religious teachings are at least in keeping with the laws of nature and the considerations of right and wrong.

5. Moreover, it is scientifically substantiated that sexual intercourse per anum is clearly contrary to the laws of biology and the human anatomy. According to medical science, there is a network of sphincter and other muscle groups surrounding the anal canal, carefully designed by our Creator to ensure efficient elimination of faecal matter from the human body.[122] Thus, these muscles collaborate or interface to provide the delicate balance between bowel continence and elimination of human waste.[123] They were constructed by the Master Designer to be primarily outward contracting for the purpose of elimination of human excrement. It is therefore illogical and an obvious health hazard for the anus to be used as a point of receptivity for the male genital. On the other hand, the muscles of the vagina are predominantly inward contracting to receive the male genital in the sexual act. Our Supreme Creator, in His wisdom, knew exactly what He was doing.

6. In terms of Christian belief, there is strong prohibition against anal sexual penetration in the Levitical code (Leviticus Chapter 18 of the Holy Bible):

> **You shall not lie with a male as with a woman. It is an abomination. Nor shall you mate with any animal, to defile yourself with it. Nor shall any woman stand before an animal to mate with it. It is perversion (vv. 22-23).**

Also, in Romans chapter 1, verses 26 and 27, the Holy Bible reveals:

---

[122] The Global Library of Women's Medicine. "Anal Incontinence." The International Federation of Gynaecology and Obstetrics (FIGO) https://www.glowm.com/section_view/heading/Anal%20Incontinence/item/72.
[123] Ibid.

[26]For this reason God gave them up to vile passions. For even their women exchanged the natural use for what is against nature. [27]Likewise also the men, leaving the natural use of the woman, burned in their lust for one another, men with men committing what is shameful, and receiving in themselves the penalty of their error which was due.

For the purpose of this discussion, "vile passions" means "passions of dishonour," the literal translation from the Greek language. In the light of the foregoing, therefore, this writer insists that the issue of buggery could not be settled as a constitutional matter merely from the standpoint of legal arguments, devoid of moral and spiritual values and the rule of law. There is overwhelming moral, ethical and spiritual preclusion to any form of same-sex affection in the Holy Bible.

7. In its April 12th, 2018 judgment, the court also made the following statement:

> At this point, the court feels compelled to state in conclusion that it is unfortunate when society in any way values a person or gives a person their identity based on their race, colour, gender, age or sexual orientation. That is not their identity. That is not their soul. That is not the sum total of their value to society or their value to themselves. . . To now deny a perceived minority their right to humanity and human dignity would be to continue this type of thinking, the type of perceived superiority based on the

genuinely held beliefs of some."[124]

Again, the undergirding principles found in the preamble of our Constitution help us to clearly define what "humanity and human dignity" is. The "genuinely held beliefs of some" is in fact what the Constitution upholds since it limits freedom by "respect for moral and spiritual values and the rule of law." Moreover, the SOA, in particular, sections 13 and 16, was sanctioned by a three-fifth majority of Parliament, seeking to adhere to the principles of the Supremacy of God, moral and spiritual values and the dignity of the human person, among other things, like the constitution says. It certainly does not appear to be deliberate on the court's part, but one is left to wonder if the "perceived superiority" to which it is referring could include Parliament.

8. By overemphasizing the plight of a minority that are said to be discriminated against, thereby ignoring the voice of the majority, one may well fall into the trap of reverse discrimination. Yes, by ignoring all the moral and spiritual values that have made us what we are as a coherent, strong and stable Republic, in preference to the wishes of a minority demanding rights that are not basic and fundamental to human society, our political, judicial and civil leaders could well be engendering reverse discrimination. In fact, by deciding that sections 13 and 16 of the SOA are unconstitutional, for the reasons given, the Court has swung the pendulum from one extreme to the next, because now the majority view, the view of the People of Trinidad and Tobago as enshrined in the Constitution, affirmed especially by the Preamble, is ignored and overridden. Given that all citizens of the Republic of Trinidad and Tobago are to be protected under the constitution, the court needed to find a balance and not go from one extreme to the other.

---

[124] In The Matter Of An Application For Constitutional Redress Under S.14 Of The Constitution Between Jason Jones and The Attorney General Of Trinidad And Tobago. April 12th, 2018, The Order, paragraph 173, p. 52. Claim No. CV2017-00720.

9. In paragraph 22 of the court's September 20th, 2018 assessment, the court in its conclusion stated:

> The defendant has failed to establish any legitimate legislative purpose in conformity with the constitution in forbidding sexual intercourse per anum between consenting adults... Born out of the abhorrence shown towards homosexuals, the section asserted sexual intercourse per anum in a category of its own. The court has already found this to be unconstitutional in relation to consenting adults.[125]

On the contrary, this writer wishes to point out here that the constitution speaks for itself in that the People of Trinidad and Tobago have already

> 'affirmed that the Nation of Trinidad and Tobago is founded upon principles that acknowledge the supremacy of God, faith in fundamental human rights and freedoms, the position of the family in a society of free men and free institutions, the dignity of the human person and the equal and inalienable rights with which all members of the human family are

---

[125] In The Matter Of An Application For Constitutional Redress Under S.14 Of The Constitution Between Jason Jones and The Attorney General Of Trinidad And Tobago. Sept. 20th, 2018, paragraph 22, p. 11. Claim No. CV2017-00720.

> endowed by their Creator'[126]
>
> and further recognise that men and institutions remain free only when freedom is founded upon respect for moral and spiritual values and the rule of law[127]; and still further.
>
> desire that their Constitution should enshrine the above-mentioned principles and beliefs and make provision for ensuring the protection in Trinidad and Tobago of fundamental human rights and freedoms.[128]

10. In the light of the provisions of the Constitution, therefore, the court could not justifiably claim that 'the defendant has failed to establish any legitimate legislative purpose in conformity with the constitution in forbidding sexual intercourse per annum between consenting adults,' since the prohibition in question is already in conformity with the Constitution. The point needs to be reiterated that the mere notion of the Supremacy of God makes it mandatory that 'fundamental human rights and freedoms, the position of the family in a society of free men and free institutions, the dignity of the human person and the equal and inalienable rights with which all members of the human family are endowed by their Creator' must all be rooted in that truism itself. It must be reiterated that the Constitution makes it absolutely clear that 'men and institutions remain free only when freedom is founded upon respect for moral and spiritual values and the rule of law.'

---

[126] Constitution of the Republic of Trinidad and Tobago Act, Chapter 1:01 Act 4 of 1976. Preamble, Clause (a). Laws of Trinidad and Tobago, Ministry of Legal Affairs. https://www.oas.org/dil/Constitution_of_the_of_Trinidad_Tobago_Act_Act.pdf.
[127] Ibid, Clause (d).
[128] Ibid, Clause (e).

11. The main problem with the court's judgment, as hinted before, is that it sought to establish the unconstitutionality of the SOA "forbidding sexual intercourse per anum between consenting adults," while at the same time ignoring "moral and spiritual values," essential qualifiers for determining "free men and free institutions" under the Constitution of the Republic of Trinidad and Tobago. Thus, by looking at sexual intercourse per anum through lens devoid of moral and spiritual values, the court was left with no choice but to see the prohibition of sexual intercourse per anum in the SOA as being "Born out of the abhorrence shown towards homosexuals." This is an unfounded assumption since the premise of the court's argument does not embrace factors as fundamental as moral and spiritual beliefs.

12. The court concedes at paragraph 25 in its September 20th, 2018 assessment that 'Parliament cannot legislate contrary to the provisions of the constitution.' Indeed, when viewed through the lens of moral and spiritual values (imperative limiters of freedom in the constitution), contrary to the line of argumentation of the court (paragraphs 22 to 25 of the September 20th, 2018 court order), Parliament, in fact, by way of sections 13 and 16 of the SOA, cannot be said to have legislated contrary to the provisions of the Constitution. Parliament, rather, seems to be in full compliance with the constitution.

13. Closely associated with the foregoing, the court in its April 12th conclusion, paragraph 174, states:

> However, this conclusion is a recognition that the beliefs of some, by definition, is not the belief of all and, in the Republic of Trinidad and Tobago, all are protected, and are entitled to be

protected, under the constitution. As a result, the court must and will uphold the constitution to recognize the dignity of even one citizen whose rights and freedoms have been invalidly taken away.

While the court should be commended for being concerned about the dignity, rights and freedoms of even one citizen, one is again constrained to note the preamble: 'men and institutions remain free only when freedom is founded upon respect for moral and spiritual values and the rule of law' (clause (d)). Thus, "all" can only be protected or entitled to be protected under the constitution in the circumstances of respect for moral and spiritual values and the rule of law.

14. Again, in its April 12th, 2018 deliberations, the court reveals a presupposition which no doubt would have strongly influenced its judgment:

> There is no doubt that maintaining the traditional family and values that represent society are important concepts but those words have now to be adapted to a different world than medieval and Victorian times.'[129]

Are we now being asked to dispense with "traditional family and values that represent society" simply because of what is now trending, regardless of how detrimental the latter is to the stability of the family or human society as a whole? Should not responsible leaders of our society rather carefully

---

[129] In The Matter Of An Application For Constitutional Redress Under S.14 Of The Constitution Between Jason Jones and The Attorney General Of Trinidad And Tobago. April 12th, 2018, The Order, paragraph 169, p. 52. Claim No. CV2017-00720.

examine, consider and seek to correct the causal factors of unnatural sexual behaviours and attitudes rather than merely package the latter and present them to society, whether or not they promote "the moral and spiritual values and the rule of law" of our society? Much introspection is needed here. For the well-being of society, should we be majoring in descriptive or prescriptive ethics? Which would benefit our children, our teenagers, adults and our society more? We owe it to ourselves and posterity to make the right judgment here.

15. The court expands the expression of its presupposition concerning the family in paragraph 170 of the April 12th hearing:

> What is a traditional family? If it is limited to a mother, father and children, then, once again, the rationale for keeping that template is no longer sufficiently important as the rationale for denying the claimant's fundamental rights. For example, single-parent families are becoming a norm which is unsettling to many traditionalists despite its reality. As has been shown, the values that represent society have dramatically changed as democratic societies have now moved to accept that laws such as these under scrutiny are no longer necessary.

This is certainly a case of denying the fundamental rights

of the majority to accommodate the rights of the minority although the latter may not be adhering to freedom 'founded upon respect for moral and spiritual values and the rule of law.' The value of the traditional or natural family does not diminish in proportion to the proliferation of single-parent or other non-ideal forms. What becomes a norm is not necessarily the right or the best thing for humanity. Rather, society should be taking note of the serious drawbacks to the mental, psychological, social and even psycho-somatic health of contemporary society owing to the mushrooming of alternative family forms. Again, responsible Government leaders owe it to themselves and to those that they lead to search out and remove causalities of deviant behaviour, rather than remain oblivious of the latter and seek to make redundant fundamental values that underpin our very existence as a civil society. Trinidad and Tobago is a sovereign state and should not be dependent upon what other democracies accept or reject as a way of determining what is good or bad for us. We boast of independence, then let us act as if we are independent. Much deeper self-analysis is imperative if anarchy or lawlessness is not to break down our doors and reduce society to the law of the jungle.

16. I submit that the decision of the court on the buggery law would have far-reaching and dire consequences for our twin island Republic of Trinidad and Tobago if not rescinded by a higher authority. We refer back to one of the focal points of the Preamble—'the equal and inalienable rights with which all members of the human family are endowed by their Creator.' It must be noted that in relation to the preamble of our Constitution, "equal rights" cannot be unqualified and carte blanche, or else every conceivable wish, deep feeling or orientation would have to be honoured by law, regardless of their merit or demerit, thus generating a free-for-all and ungovernable society. Again, to be correct, equal rights can only be tenable as human rights when aligned to sound moral values, as enshrined in our Constitution, and when

such freedoms, I repeat, are 'founded upon respect for moral and spiritual values and the rule of law'. If not, we could be in danger of creating a state in which the very attempt to enforce law results in the accommodation of irresponsible and counterproductive behaviour under the banner of "equal rights," creating anarchy. Is this what we want for Trinidad and Tobago?

17. We believe that it is the quest for equalizing the sexes in terms of roles and functions by the feminist movement in the late 60's and early 70's that has largely propelled the redefinition of gender and proliferated a spectrum of "gender types." Gayle Rubin's position that feminism should aim at creating a "genderless" (not necessarily sexless) society where one's anatomy is "irrelevant to who one is, what one does, and with whom one makes love" confirms the foregoing.[130] Ironically, the so-called gender types uncannily superimpose themselves on sex (known as biologically fixed), drastically changing sexual norms, attitudes and behaviours. How subtle!

18. We believe that God created man and woman equal in value from the beginning, so that the woman was not an afterthought of God. The Genesis account (Gen. 2:7-18) shows that God made the man functional first mainly to establish male leadership and avoid leadership controversy. Our Creator made the woman as an invaluable complement to the fulfilment of His own vision for the human race. Thus, we were designed as male (Heb. *zakar* = sharp male organ) and female (Heb. *nekevah* = pierced, womb or opening) for the main purpose of procreation (Gen. 1:26-28). Pleasure was on the cards (the human anatomy being endowed with all kinds of sexual pleasure points), but the main purpose was to be procreation.

---

[130] Gayle Rubin, 1975, "The Traffic in Women: Notes on the 'Political Economy' of Sex", in Toward an Anthropology of Women, R. Reiter (ed.), New York: Monthly Review Press. https://purpleprosearchive.wordpress.com/2009/01/30/gayle-rubin-the-traffic-in-women-1975/

19. Overemphasis on human pleasure lays the foundation for exploitation and misapplication of human sexuality as is now evident, leading to unwholesome sexual practices.

20. If the Constitution of the Republic of Trinidad and Tobago is founded on the principles of the supremacy of God, among other things, then that becomes the basis on which we should build the nation. We should then be patterning our nation after the creation model, particularly as our Constitution seeks to enshrine, among other things, the dignity of the human person and the equal and inalienable rights with which all members of the human family are endowed by their Creator.

21. With regard to the purpose of the law, the Holy Bible affirms that the law (a body of principles for preserving human life) was introduced "because of transgressions" (Gal. 3:19). God introduced the law to prevent violation of His unchanging standard of truth and morality essential for the stability and integrity of any society. The preamble of our constitution says nothing essentially different, in that the latter would "make provision for ensuring the protection in Trinidad and Tobago of fundamental human rights and freedoms."[131] In other words, the law is supposed to prevent society from self-destructing. Reference to the "Supremacy of God" in our Preamble is testimony to the fact that original framers of our constitution knew that law originated from God. The law then must not be made to accommodate all forms of wrong when it was designed to eliminate the latter.

22. By divorcing morality from law, as the court implies, one is treating law as if it were separate and superior to morality and not a companion of it. Ultimate chaos and disorder are the inevitable results, basically opposite to what the

---

[131] Constitution of the Republic of Trinidad and Tobago Act, Chapter 1:01 Act 4 of 1976. Preamble, Clause (e). Laws of Trinidad and Tobago, Ministry of Legal Affairs. https://www.oas.org/dil/Constitution_of_the_of_Trinidad_Tobago_Act_Act.pdf.

Constitution pledges to uphold. Is this what we want for our people? If we are not careful, we could be heading down a slippery slope fast, so to speak, as a nation.

23. In several jurisdictions where the buggery law has been decriminalized, a domino effect has begun. First of all, the mad rush for the fallacious "equal rights" has already resulted in a never-ending LGBTQQIP2SAA... acronym, since every request for "equal rights" must now be accommodated. This inevitably opens up the door to the eventual sanctioning of incest, paedophilia, child pornography, bestiality, gender fluidity, pangenderism, queer imaginations such as some adults wanting to be recognized as children again (complete with pampers and bottles), a mother and daughter demanding the rights to be lovers, a son and mother as well, brother and sister, sister and sister, and any imagination of the mind possible. In reality, once you allow one unnatural and lawfully prohibited practice, how can you say no to the rest? Can our nation bear the cost of this melee? We have a responsibility of fixing our own house, not accommodating other people's whims and fancies. We must take the necessary steps now.

24. I wish to advance that if the LBGTQQIP2SAA... community becomes a protected class in Trinidad and Tobago, as is in the case of other jurisdictions such as Canada, some parts of the United States, Demark, and Britain, further demands for so-called "equality" will fan out into the following:

    A. **The introduction of anti-discrimination laws, based mainly on one nuance of discrimination** — "the practice of unfairly treating a person or group differently from other people or groups of people"—deliberately ignoring other nuances of the word. For example, it would be absurd and a violation of a person's fundamental human rights to label that person as discriminating if that person distinguishes good sexual practices from bad sexual practices and point out the possible dangers to individuals, families and society at large.

B. **Removal of parental rights.** In Canada and in the State of California, it has already been made law that a child has the right to choose his or her sexual orientation. Those jurisdictions also stipulate that it is illegal for parents to attempt to dissuade their child from their perceived imaginations and feelings. Any parent so indicted could lose custody of their child and serve jail time. In many cases, many children have been persuaded by teachers in school to give up their natural identity; girls are coached and even coerced to insist that they be called "he" and boys that they be called "she." In some cases, a single person may insist that he or she be called "them." What utter confusion! The average child has a built-in sensitivity as to how to interpret his or her anatomy, who he or she is without having to be told. Yet there is a campaign to convince our kids that they could be anything they feel like in spite of the genitals they carry. This inevitably is resulting in utter confusion, manic depression and suicide. Can we survive as a civilization in this quagmire of stupefaction? Is this what we want for our society? Can we as adults live with the guilt of disorienting the psyches of our posterity, innocent and precious young minds who we hope would take the reins of leadership after us?

C. **The wholesale acceptance of gender as a "social construct"[132] (sociological opinion and speculation) rather than reference to an empirical distinction between male and female based on sex and sexual behaviour (biological or scientific facts).** Reference is made to the difference between the definition of gender in the Rome Statute of the International Criminal Court 1998 [133] and that of the 4th World Conference on Women,

---

[132] 4th World Conference on Women, Beijing 1995
[133] Rome Statute of the International Criminal Court 1998.

Beijing 1995 (three years before).[134] In other words, when put to the real test of life, gender as a social construct does not stand up. Biology and the hard sciences cannot accommodate gender as a social construct. Have we chosen then to deliberately go against the laws of nature and the precepts of the Supreme God to satisfy the whims and fancies of the few? Can we bare the eventual consequences of this as a society? We believe that gender is a fact of nature and therefore cannot be redefined no more than the sun or moon could be redefined; only a concept can be redefined. Further, no world authority, be it the United Nations, PAHO, UNICEF, OAS, the European Union, the feminist movement, nobody, could claim the notion of gender as its own; it follows that none has the right to alter its meaning and make it fit into his or her own agenda. This sounds like a type of plagiarism. Our own professors would expel students from their institutions for such practice.

D. **The demand for same-sex "marriage."** This has been the eventual result in virtually all the jurisdictions where the buggery laws have been altered or removed to allow for sodomy. Our Constitution does not allow for such unnatural and undignified activity since it has affirmed that the Nation of Trinidad and Tobago is

> "founded upon principles that acknowledge the supremacy of God, faith in fundamental human rights and freedoms, the position of the family in a society of free men and free institutions, the dignity of the human person and the equal and inalienable

---

[134] 4th World Conference on Women, Beijing 1995

rights with which all members of the human family are endowed by their Creator . . . recognise that men and institutions remain free only when freedom is founded upon respect for moral and spiritual values and the rule of law."

Moreover, our Constitution is indeed conscious of its enshrinement of the above-mentioned principles and beliefs and make provision for ensuring the protection in Trinidad and Tobago of fundamental human rights and freedoms.[135] As Christians, we reject the notion of same-sex union or marriage on the basis of the Levitical code in Leviticus chapter 18 as well as the Apostle Paul's prognosis in Romans chapter 1:18-32.

We believe that same-sex marriage is therefore a desecration of the marriage institution ordained by our Supreme Creator. Moreover, such a sacrilegious practice cannot be rightfully accommodated by a constitution that "is founded upon principles that acknowledge the supremacy of God." Again, to us, it seems unconstitutional to make any alteration to our constitution, or enact legislation, when doing so, that would be contrary to the principles on which the very constitution is founded.

E. **The eventual legal indictment and persecution of all faith-based persons** who would as much as point out (a form of proper discrimination), by reason of conscientious objection (a human right), that the practice of homosexuality or similar unnatural practice,

---

[135] Constitution of the Republic of Trinidad and Tobago Act, Chapter 1:01 Act 4 of 1976. Preamble, Clause (d). Laws of Trinidad and Tobago, Ministry of Legal Affairs. https://www.oas.org/dil/Constitution_of_the_of_Trinidad_Tobago_Act_Act.pdf.

is something of bad quality for our society, our children and the continuity and survival of civilization as a whole. This is the general trend in other jurisdictions.

F. **The health risks and the associated economic cost in dealing with the increased incidence of HIV/Aids and other STDs.** According to K. H. Mayer's abstract on "Sexually Transmitted Diseases in Men Who Have Sex with Men,"[136]

> Men who have sex with men (MSM) have increased rates of human immunodeficiency virus (HIV) infection and sexually transmitted diseases (STDs) compared with demographically matched controls.

Another study by Vanderbilt University Medical Center reveals, among several high-risk health findings, that: "Gay men are at high risk for getting the human papilloma virus (HPV), which can cause anal papilloma and certain types of anal cancers" and that "Men who have sex with men have higher rates of depression and anxiety compared to others . . . As a result, gay teenagers and young adults have an increased risk of suicide."[137]

Based on a 2008 study, Matt Slick identifies a mental health risk, among other things, in that "homosexuals are about 50% more likely to suffer from depression and engage in substance abuse than the rest of the

---

[136] Kenneth H. Mayer. 2011. "Sexually Transmitted Diseases in Men Who Have Sex With Men," in the Clinical Infectious Disease: an official publication of the infectious Diseases Society of America. December; 53 Suppl 3:S79-83.

[137] Vanderbilt University Medical Center. https://www.vumc.org/lgbtq/health-concerns-msm

population."[138]

In addition, the level of sexual promiscuity among gays is extremely alarming and a risk to any society. Weinberg and Bell, in their book, "Homosexualities: A Study of Diversity Among Men and women," disclose some eye-opening statistics, revealing the following, among other things:

> 75 percent of self-identified, white, gay men admitted to having sex with more than 100 different males in their lifetime: 15 percent claimed 100-249 sex partners; 17 percent claimed 250-499; 15 percent claimed 500-999; and 28 percent claimed more than 1,000 lifetime male sex partners.[139]

According to a GPL Atlantic press release dated June 2001, the following statistics were revealed:

> HIV/AIDS cost Canadians more than $2 billion in 1999 in direct and indirect costs. Health care costs accounted for about $560 million; prevention, research and supports to AIDS victims for about $40 million;

---

[138] Cathleen Gilbert, LifeSiteNews.com, Sept. 17th, 2008

[139] Martin S. Weinberg And Alan Paul Bell, 'Homosexualities: A Study of Diversity among Men and Women' (Touchstone, 1979) p. 308. In Marriage Alliance. http://www.marriagealliance.com.au/martin_s_weinberg_and_alan_paul_bell_homosexualities_a_study_of_diversity_among_men_and_women_touchstone_1979_p_308.

and lost economic production due to premature death and disability for nearly $1.5 billion.[140]

Are the foregoing the kinds of statistics that we would like to promote in our nation? The economic burden carried by this nation in terms of crime is already overbearing. Are the foregoing statistics not glaring enough to cause Government to curtail the free-for-all, promiscuous and reckless lifestyles now being proposed? If we as a nation shut our eyes and plunge into this glaring fiery furnace, then posterity should have the right to condemn all of us for our ignorance and conceitedness.

25. It should also be noted that at a three-day caucus of Faith Based Organizations organized by the Government of Trinidad and Tobago in early 2015 at the now Raddison Hotel, all the heads of religions present, inclusive of several non-Christian denominations representing over nine hundred thousand (900,000) of the citizens of the Republic of Trinidad and Tobago) unanimously agreed to recognize the definition of "Gender" established by the Rome Statute 1998 and not that of the Beijing Convention 1995. The general consensus was that any homosexual accommodation by the political powers that be would open the floodgate to lawlessness and a destruction of the moral fabric of our society.

26. Again, the following fact must be carefully noted:

"The European Court for Human Rights has ruled that same-sex 'marriages' are not considered a human right, making it clear that homosexual partnerships do

---

[140] GPLAtlantic. "HIV/AIDS Costs Canada $2 Billion a Year." June 2001. http://www.gpiatlantic.org/releases/pr_cost_aids.htm.

not in fact equal marriages between a man and a woman."[141]

Then why should any nation force the issue? Are we merely following popular wrong or should we be exercising sound judgment for the advancement of our people?

27. Pope Francis' comments in the case of Kim Davis, a Kentucky Law clerk who had refused to issue a marriage license to a homosexual couple in 2015, should be carefully noted.[142]

28. In conclusion, having regard to the foregoing, we hereby petition and implore our Honourable Prime Minister and Attorney General in particular and the Government of Trinidad and Tobago in general to ensure that a strong appeal is made to the relevant courts to overturn the recent High Court order on the buggery law. We posit that the latter should remain among our major laws to ensure that our legislation enshrines "the principles of the supremacy of God, faith in the fundamental human rights and freedoms, the position of the family in a society of free men and free institutions" as clearly delineated in our Constitution. It is "only when freedom is founded upon respect for moral and spiritual values and the rule of law," as well as "the dignity of the human person and the equal and inalienable rights with which all members of the human family are endowed by their Creator,"[143] can this nation thrive. In so doing, our Constitution would "make provision for ensuring the protection in Trinidad and Tobago of fundamental human rights and freedoms"[144] and in the process, promote the sound values of the natural family that have kept this nation free and safe for all these years. Indeed,

---

[141] LifeSiteNews, https://www.lifesitenews.com/news/european-human-rights-court-rejects-gay-marriage, Strasbourg, June 29, 2016
[142] Pope Francis. Sept. 28, 2015: *Pope: Workers have 'Human Right' to Refuse Same-sex Marriage Licenses*; NBC report by Alastair Jamieson.
[143] Preamble, Constitution of the Republic of Trinidad and Tobago.
[144] Ibid., clause (e)

it is these strong moral, ethical and spiritual values that have been the foundation for our continued advancement as a nation.

14

KNOW THE TRUTH AND NOTHING BUT THE TRUTH

It is fitting that in this last chapter I address the issue of truth since the lack thereof seems to be the main contributor to the mushrooming of liberal ideologies and philosophies of postmodernism. Indeed, this key deficiency has given rise to all the self-propagated and subjective concepts and practices objected to by this author within the pages of this book. Truth is one of the most elusive targets of human history. This is mainly because man has been searching for it in the wrong place. It could not be birthed in the mind of man. It is not a product of philosophy so as to be found in Plato or Aristotle. If that were the case, there would be no truth, since man's many and varied theories would have cancelled out one another, for every man thinks differently.

The biblical position is that there is a Creator that exists before the human mind and human reasoning. He is the One that is there and always will be there. He is the one that mankind has come and met here. If one is looking for the truth, therefore, one would have to look to that unchanging Source. It is only logical that if one is looking to a shifting or changeable source for truth, then if that "truth" could ever be found it could never really be truth, since truth, in order to be truth, must be unchangeable. Yes, by its very nature (and that has nothing to do with whether one is a Christian or not), truth must be represented by an unchangeable source. Thus, truth will have to emerge from the Creator Himself (the only unchangeable cause) and not merely an idea or thought. In fact the Bible personifies truth as God Himself.

This is why God instructed Moses to identify Him as "The I Am" when he went to deliver the Children of Israel from the hand of Pharaoh in the land of Egypt. The expression "The I Am" literally means "The One who always is." In Exodus 3:14, we read, *"And God said to Moses, 'I AM WHO I AM.' And He said, 'Thus you shall say to the children of Israel, I AM has sent me to you.'"* The Hebrew expression for "I am who I am" is *eyeh asher ehyeh.* Jesus in His self-disclosure in John's Gospel chapter 14 and verse 6 identifies Himself with the deity of God the Father when he says pointedly: *"I am the way, the truth, and the life: no man cometh unto the Father, but by me."* In other words truth is not what is found in human reasoning but is itself a personification—the person of Jesus, "the express image" of the Father Himself (Heb. 1:3)

One would recall that Pontius Pilot, the Roman official at the trial of Jesus (recorded in John chapter 18 and verse 37) had asked Jesus: "What is truth?' Jesus never answered; one reason may well be that Pilate asked the wrong question. He should have asked "Who is truth?" I am sure Jesus would have been delighted to disclose "The Truth" to him.

James W. Sire, in his book, Naming the Elephant: Worldview as a Concept, refers to God the Creator as the "Prime Reality" from whom epistemology (the theory of knowledge) emanates. He argues that ontology (the theory of being) must therefore precede epistemology.[145] In other words, one's concept of life may not be authentic if it has no legitimate grounds. It is easy for one

---

[145] James Sire, Naming the Elephant: Worldview as a Concept (InterVarsity Press, Downers Grove, 2004), 51-56.

to incur serious blunders and ridiculous *faux pas* if one ignores truth. That is why the Bible states emphatically the existence of God and does not try to prove it.[146]

From the foregoing position, one should be able to see that the basic confusion in human reasoning behind the gender crisis has stemmed mainly from the quest for knowledge (epistemological considerations) without first acknowledging "Who or What is." I reiterate that truth must be what we all came and met rather than what we conceptualize. That is the reason why so many have been disillusioned and are coming up with unnatural, coerced and imposed notions of life. Some are constrained to alter natural laws and moral standards that are necessary for a stable human society, that which God intended from the beginning. A poor perception of truth is what has resulted in so many fallacious arguments in this gender crisis, even the distortion of human rights itself.

If the reader is honest enough to acknowledge his or her error in contributing to the present gender crisis, and is willing to acknowledge the Ultimate Reality—God—as truth, then there is hope for humanity to be guided to its ideal destiny. If not, there is danger of sure peril, confusion and anarchy. Then truth would always be elusive and man would continue to be disillusioned. Here is the opportunity for you to shift your position and no longer be misguided. Know the Truth and nothing but the Truth and let the I Am guide you from henceforth.

We must never be ashamed or be fearful of the truth, for here is what the psalmist assures us in Psalm 91:4-8:

> He shall cover you with His feathers, and under His wings you shall take refuge; His truth shall be your shield and buckler. [5] You shall not be afraid of the terror by night, nor of the arrow that flies by day, [6] nor of the pestilence that walks in darkness, nor of the destruction that lays waste at noonday. [7] A thousand may fall at

---

[146] Genesis 1:1: "In the beginning God created the heavens and the earth."

your side, and ten thousand at your right hand; but it shall not come near you. [8] **Only with your eyes shall you look, and see the reward of the wicked.**

In other words, if we speak the truth and nothing but the truth, it shall become our shield and buckler and our defence. Therefore we shall not fear terror or other forms of attack. In fact, our enemies shall all fall at our left and our right, and shall not overpower us. Our eyes shall see the fate of the wicked. To God be the glory. He indeed is the great I AM.

BIBLIOGRAPHY

Armas, Kat. "What Does 'Helper' Really Mean?"
https://katarmas.com/blog/2018/8/3/what-does-helper-really-mean. 06/28/19.

Benner, Jeff A. "What is a 'help meet'?" Ancient Hebrew Research Center: Ploughing through History from the Aleph to the Tav.
https://www.ancient-hebrew.org/articles_helpmeet.html. 06/28/19.

Beres, Derek. "The Decline of Men: How the American Male Is Tuning Out, Giving Up, and Flipping Off His Future." 18 March, 2009. *Popmatters*.
https://www.popmatters.com/66805-the-decline-of-men-how-the-american-male-is-tuning-out-giving-up-and--2496094535.html. 09/19/19.

Brown, Francis, S.R. Driver, Charles A. Briggs. Hebrew and English Lexicon of the Old Testament.

Cambridge Dictionary.

Duncan, Joseph Vernon. 2002. The Zakar Man: Male Man in Full Flight. Zakar Productions TNT Ltd, Arima, Trinidad.

English Oxford Dictionary

English Oxford Living Dictionaries.

Encyclopaedia Britannica.

Fehr, Carla. 2011. "Feminist Philosophy of Biology." Standard Encylopedia of Philosophy.
https://plato.stanford.edu/entries/feminist-philosophy-biology/. 06/29/19.

Free Thinkers. "Locations of Obelisks Around the world,"
https://www.tapatalk.com/groups/free_thinkers/locations- of-obelisks-around-the-world-t6278.html. 09/19/19

Herek, Gregory. 2017. "The Father of 'Homophobia': George Wineberg (1929-2017)." *Beyond Homophobia*, a weblog about sexual orientation, prejudice, science and policy.
https://herek.net/blog/the-father-of-homophobia-george-weinberg-1929-2017/. 07/02/19

Hutchings, Noah W. 1990. The Persian Gulf Crisis and the Final Fall of Babylon. Oklahoma: Hearthstone Publishing.

Little, William and Ron McGivern. *Introduction to Sociology—* 1st Canadian Edition. OpenStax College. Creative Commons Attribution 4.0 International License.

https://my.uopeople.edu/pluginfile.php/57436/mod_book/chapter/37634/SOC1502.Textbook.pdf. 06/30/19.

Learn Religions. "The Story of Jezebel in the Bible: A Worshipper of Baal and Enemy of God." Updated February 23, 2019.
https://www.learnreligions.com/who-was-jezebel-2076726. 06/30/19.

Makola, Mari. 2017. "Feminist Perspectives on Sex and Gender." Standard Encyclopedia of Psychology.
https://plato.stanford.edu/entries/feminism-gender/ 07/02/19.

Merriam Webster

Merriam-Webster Word Central dictionary.

Mowczko, Marg. "A Suitable Helper (in Hebrew)." *Exploring the Biblical Theology of Christian Egalitarianism.* March 8, 2010. Accessed June 28, 2019.
https://margmowczko.com/a-suitable-helper. 06/28/19.

Online Etymology Dictionary

Onlymyhealth. "Process of Construction to Birth." Feb. 14th, 2013.
https://www.onlymyhealth.com/process-conception-birth-1345140048 06/28/19.

Oosterveld, Valerie "The Definition of 'Gender' in the Rome Statute of the International Criminal Court: A Step Forward or Back for International Criminal Justice?"
http://wikigender.org/wp-content/uploads/files/Definition_of_gender_

in_the_Rome_Statute.pdf. 06/28/19.

Scrum_Jet. "Gayle Rubin, The Traffic in Women (1975)" (blog) January 30, 2009.
https://purpleprosearchive.wordpress.com/2009/01/30/gayle-rubin-the-traffic-in-women-1975/. 07/02/19

Sire, James. 2004. *Naming the Elephant: Worldview as a Concept.* Downers Grove; InterVarsity Press.

Spilman, M. A. "Feminist Ideology in the United States: Its Development from 1966-70 as the indicator of a general social movement." Contemporary Crises. June 1978, Vol. 2, Issue 2. pp 195-208.
https://link.springer.com/article/10.1007/BF02741931 06/28/19.

Step into the Glory from Genesis to Revelation. "Discover the Biblical Character of Nimrod," https://stepintothestory.ca/know-nimrod-married-mother/. 09/19/19.

Strong's Exhaustive Concordance of the Bible.

The Global Library of Women's Medicine. "Anal Incontinence." The International Federation of Gynaecology and Obstetrics (FIGO).
https://www.glowm.com/section_view/heading/Anal%20Incontinence/item/72. 07/02/19.

The World Health Organization. "Sexual and Reproductive Health,"
https://www.who.int/reproductivehealth/topics/sexual_health/sh_definitions/en/. 06/28/19.

"Trinidad and Tobago Draft National Gender Policy and Action Plan." 2004. Ministry of Community Development, Culture and Gender Affairs/Centre for Gender and Development Studies, University of the West Indies. In collaboration with the United Nations Development Programme and the CARICOM Gender Equality Programme, CIDA.

Webster's Dictionary 1828—Online Edition.

Weinberg, George. 1972. Society and the Healthy Homosexual. New York: St. Martin's Press

Weinberg, George,. "Love is Conspirational, Deviant and Magcal," *interview by Raj Ayyar; GayToday.com.* www.gaytoday.com/interview/110102in.asp. 07/02/19.

Made in the USA
Columbia, SC
17 September 2020